D1537033

THIS IS YOUR **PASSBOOK**® FOR ...

LICENSED PRACTICAL NURSE

NATIONAL LEARNING CORPORATION®
passbooks.com

PASSBOOK® SERIES

THE *PASSBOOK® SERIES* has been created to prepare applicants and candidates for the ultimate academic battlefield – the examination room.

At some time in our lives, each and every one of us may be required to take an examination – for validation, matriculation, admission, qualification, registration, certification, or licensure.

Based on the assumption that every applicant or candidate has met the basic formal educational standards, has taken the required number of courses, and read the necessary texts, the *PASSBOOK® SERIES* furnishes the one special preparation which may assure passing with confidence, instead of failing with insecurity. Examination questions – together with answers – are furnished as the basic vehicle for study so that the mysteries of the examination and its compounding difficulties may be eliminated or diminished by a sure method.

This book is meant to help you pass your examination provided that you qualify and are serious in your objective.

The entire field is reviewed through the huge store of content information which is succinctly presented through a provocative and challenging approach – the question-and-answer method.

A climate of success is established by furnishing the correct answers at the end of each test.

You soon learn to recognize types of questions, forms of questions, and patterns of questioning. You may even begin to anticipate expected outcomes.

You perceive that many questions are repeated or adapted so that you can gain acute insights, which may enable you to score many sure points.

You learn how to confront new questions, or types of questions, and to attack them confidently and work out the correct answers.

You note objectives and emphases, and recognize pitfalls and dangers, so that you may make positive educational adjustments.

Moreover, you are kept fully informed in relation to new concepts, methods, practices, and directions in the field.

You discover that you arre actually taking the examination all the time: you are preparing for the examination by "taking" an examination, not by reading extraneous and/or supererogatory textbooks.

In short, this PASSBOOK®, used directedly, should be an important factor in helping you to pass your test.

LICENSED PRACTICAL NURSES

NATURE OF THE WORK

Licensed practical nurses help care for the physically or mentally ill and infirm. Under the direction of physicians and registered nurses, they provide nursing care that requires technical knowledge but not the professional training of a registered nurse. In California and Texas, licensed practical nurses are called licensed vocational nurses.

In hospitals, licensed practical nurses provide much of the bedside care needed by patients. They take and record temperatures and blood pressures, change dressings, administer certain prescribed medicines, and help bed patients with bathing and other personal hygiene. They assist physicians and registered nurses in examining patients and in carrying out nursing procedures. They also assist in the delivery, care, and feeding of infants, and help registered nurses in recovery rooms by reporting any adverse changes in patients. Some licensed practical nurses help supervise hospital attendants.

Licensed practical nurses who work in private homes provide mainly day-to-day patient care that seldom involves highly technical procedures or complicated equipment. In addition to providing nursing care, they may prepare meals and care for the patient's comfort and morale. They also teach family members how to perform simple nursing tasks.

In doctors' offices and in clinics, licensed practical nurses prepare patients for examination and treatment. They also may make appointments and record information about patients.

PLACES OF EMPLOYMENT

About 430,000 persons — the great majority of them women — worked as licensed practical nurses. Hospitals employed about three-fifths of all licensed practical nurses. Most of the other worked in nursing homes, clinics, doctors' offices, sanatoriums, and other long-term care facilities. Many worked or public health agencies and welfare and religious organizations. Some were self-employed, working in hospitals or the homes of their patients.

TRAINING, OTHER QUALIFICATIONS, AND ADVANCEMENT

All States and the District of Columbia regulate the reparation and licensing of practical nurses. To be licensed, students must complete a course of instruction in practical nursing that has been approved by the State board of nursing and pass a licensing examination.

Educational requirements for enrollment in State-approved training programs range from completion of eighth or ninth grade to high school graduation. Many schools do not require completion of high school but give preference to graduates. Physical examinations and aptitude tests are usually required.

Nearly 1,300 State-approved programs provided practical nursing training. Public schools offered more than half of these programs as part of their vocational and adult education programs. Other programs were available at junior colleges, local hospitals, health agencies, and private educational institutions.

Practical nurse training programs are generally one year long and include both classroom study and clinical practice. Classroom instruction covers nursing concepts and principles and related subjects, including anatomy, physiology, medical-surgical nursing, administration of drugs, nutrition, first aid and community health. Students learn to apply their skill to an actual nursing situation through supervised hospital work.

Aspiring licensed practical nurses should have a deep concern for human welfare. They must be emotionally stable because working with sick and injured people sometimes can be upsetting.

As part of a health-care team, they must be able to follow orders and work under close supervision. Good health is very important, as is the physical stamina needed to work while standing up a great deal.

Advancement opportunities are limited without additional training. In-service educational programs prepare some licensed practical nurses for work in specialized areas. There are also some career ladder programs. Under this concept, nurses' aides attend training to become licensed practical nurses (LPN's) while continuing to work part-time. Similarly, LPN's may prepare to become registered nurses while they continue to work part-time.

EMPLOYMENT OUTLOOK

The employment outlook for licensed practical nurses is expected to be very good [through the late 1990's]. Employment is expected to continue to rise very rapidly [through the late 1990's] in response to a growing population, the increasing ability of persons to pay for health care, and the continuing expansion of public and private health insurance plans. Jobs will be created also as licensed practical nurses take over duties previously performed by registered nurses. Also, thousands of newly licensed practical nurses will be needed each year to replace those who die, retire, or leave the occupation for other reasons.

WORKING CONDITIONS

Many hospitals give periodic pay increases after specific periods of satisfactory service. Some hospitals provide free lodging and laundering of uniforms. Practical nurses generally work 40 hours a week, but often this workweek includes some work at night and on weekends and holidays. Many hospitals provide paid holidays and vacations, health insurance, and pension plans.

In private homes, licensed practical nurses usually work 8 to 12 hours a day and go home at night.

HOW TO TAKE A TEST

I. YOU MUST PASS AN EXAMINATION

A. WHAT EVERY CANDIDATE SHOULD KNOW

Examination applicants often ask us for help in preparing for the written test. What can I study in advance? What kinds of questions will be asked? How will the test be given? How will the papers be graded?

As an applicant for a civil service examination, you may be wondering about some of these things. Our purpose here is to suggest effective methods of advance study and to describe civil service examinations.

Your chances for success on this examination can be increased if you know how to prepare. Those "pre-examination jitters" can be reduced if you know what to expect. You can even experience an adventure in good citizenship if you know why civil service exams are given.

B. WHY ARE CIVIL SERVICE EXAMINATIONS GIVEN?

Civil service examinations are important to you in two ways. As a citizen, you want public jobs filled by employees who know how to do their work. As a job seeker, you want a fair chance to compete for that job on an equal footing with other candidates. The best-known means of accomplishing this two-fold goal is the competitive examination.

Exams are widely publicized throughout the nation. They may be administered for jobs in federal, state, city, municipal, town or village governments or agencies.

Any citizen may apply, with some limitations, such as the age or residence of applicants. Your experience and education may be reviewed to see whether you meet the requirements for the particular examination. When these requirements exist, they are reasonable and applied consistently to all applicants. Thus, a competitive examination may cause you some uneasiness now, but it is your privilege and safeguard.

C. HOW ARE CIVIL SERVICE EXAMS DEVELOPED?

Examinations are carefully written by trained technicians who are specialists in the field known as "psychological measurement," in consultation with recognized authorities in the field of work that the test will cover. These experts recommend the subject matter areas or skills to be tested; only those knowledges or skills important to your success on the job are included. The most reliable books and source materials available are used as references. Together, the experts and technicians judge the difficulty level of the questions.

Test technicians know how to phrase questions so that the problem is clearly stated. Their ethics do not permit "trick" or "catch" questions. Questions may have been tried out on sample groups, or subjected to statistical analysis, to determine their usefulness.

Written tests are often used in combination with performance tests, ratings of training and experience, and oral interviews. All of these measures combine to form the best-known means of finding the right person for the right job.

II. HOW TO PASS THE WRITTEN TEST

A. NATURE OF THE EXAMINATION

To prepare intelligently for civil service examinations, you should know how they differ from school examinations you have taken. In school you were assigned certain definite pages to read or subjects to cover. The examination questions were quite detailed and usually emphasized memory. Civil service exams, on the other hand, try to discover your present ability to perform the duties of a position, plus your potentiality to learn these duties. In other words, a civil service exam attempts to predict how successful you will be. Questions cover such a broad area that they cannot be as minute and detailed as school exam questions.

In the public service similar kinds of work, or positions, are grouped together in one "class." This process is known as *position-classification*. All the positions in a class are paid according to the salary range for that class. One class title covers all of these positions, and they are all tested by the same examination.

B. FOUR BASIC STEPS

1) Study the announcement

How, then, can you know what subjects to study? Our best answer is: "Learn as much as possible about the class of positions for which you've applied." The exam will test the knowledge, skills and abilities needed to do the work.

Your most valuable source of information about the position you want is the official exam announcement. This announcement lists the training and experience qualifications. Check these standards and apply only if you come reasonably close to meeting them.

The brief description of the position in the examination announcement offers some clues to the subjects which will be tested. Think about the job itself. Review the duties in your mind. Can you perform them, or are there some in which you are rusty? Fill in the blank spots in your preparation.

Many jurisdictions preview the written test in the exam announcement by including a section called "Knowledge and Abilities Required," "Scope of the Examination," or some similar heading. Here you will find out specifically what fields will be tested.

2) Review your own background

Once you learn in general what the position is all about, and what you need to know to do the work, ask yourself which subjects you already know fairly well and which need improvement. You may wonder whether to concentrate on improving your strong areas or on building some background in your fields of weakness. When the announcement has specified "some knowledge" or "considerable knowledge," or has used adjectives like "beginning principles of..." or "advanced ... methods," you can get a clue as to the number and difficulty of questions to be asked in any given field. More questions, and hence broader coverage, would be included for those subjects which are more important in the work. Now weigh your strengths and weaknesses against the job requirements and prepare accordingly.

3) Determine the level of the position

Another way to tell how intensively you should prepare is to understand the level of the job for which you are applying. Is it the entering level? In other words, is this the position in which beginners in a field of work are hired? Or is it an intermediate or advanced level? Sometimes this is indicated by such words as "Junior" or "Senior" in the class title. Other jurisdictions use Roman numerals to designate the level – Clerk I, Clerk II, for example. The word "Supervisor" sometimes appears in the title. If the level is not indicated by the title, check the description of duties. Will you be working under very close supervision, or will you have responsibility for independent decisions in this work?

4) Choose appropriate study materials

Now that you know the subjects to be examined and the relative amount of each subject to be covered, you can choose suitable study materials. For beginning level jobs, or even advanced ones, if you have a pronounced weakness in some aspect of your training, read a modern, standard textbook in that field. Be sure it is up to date and has general coverage. Such books are normally available at your library, and the librarian will be glad to help you locate one. For entry-level positions, questions of appropriate difficulty are chosen – neither highly advanced questions, nor those too simple. Such questions require careful thought but not advanced training.

If the position for which you are applying is technical or advanced, you will read more advanced, specialized material. If you are already familiar with the basic principles of your field, elementary textbooks would waste your time. Concentrate on advanced textbooks and technical periodicals. Think through the concepts and review difficult problems in your field.

These are all general sources. You can get more ideas on your own initiative, following these leads. For example, training manuals and publications of the government agency which employs workers in your field can be useful, particularly for technical and professional positions. A letter or visit to the government department involved may result in more specific study suggestions, and certainly will provide you with a more definite idea of the exact nature of the position you are seeking.

III. KINDS OF TESTS

Tests are used for purposes other than measuring knowledge and ability to perform specified duties. For some positions, it is equally important to test ability to make adjustments to new situations or to profit from training. In others, basic mental abilities not dependent on information are essential. Questions which test these things may not appear as pertinent to the duties of the position as those which test for knowledge and information. Yet they are often highly important parts of a fair examination. For very general questions, it is almost impossible to help you direct your study efforts. What we can do is to point out some of the more common of these general abilities needed in public service positions and describe some typical questions.

1) General information

Broad, general information has been found useful for predicting job success in some kinds of work. This is tested in a variety of ways, from vocabulary lists to questions about current events. Basic background in some field of work, such as sociology or economics, may be sampled in a group of questions. Often these are principles which have become familiar to most persons through exposure rather than through formal training. It is difficult to advise you how to study for these questions; being alert to the world around you is our best suggestion.

2) Verbal ability

An example of an ability needed in many positions is verbal or language ability. Verbal ability is, in brief, the ability to use and understand words. Vocabulary and grammar tests are typical measures of this ability. Reading comprehension or paragraph interpretation questions are common in many kinds of civil service tests. You are given a paragraph of written material and asked to find its central meaning.

3) Numerical ability

Number skills can be tested by the familiar arithmetic problem, by checking paired lists of numbers to see which are alike and which are different, or by interpreting charts and graphs. In the latter test, a graph may be printed in the test booklet which you are asked to use as the basis for answering questions.

4) Observation

A popular test for law-enforcement positions is the observation test. A picture is shown to you for several minutes, then taken away. Questions about the picture test your ability to observe both details and larger elements.

5) Following directions

In many positions in the public service, the employee must be able to carry out written instructions dependably and accurately. You may be given a chart with several columns, each column listing a variety of information. The questions require you to carry out directions involving the information given in the chart.

6) Skills and aptitudes

Performance tests effectively measure some manual skills and aptitudes. When the skill is one in which you are trained, such as typing or shorthand, you can practice. These tests are often very much like those given in business school or high school courses. For many of the other skills and aptitudes, however, no short-time preparation can be made. Skills and abilities natural to you or that you have developed throughout your lifetime are being tested.

Many of the general questions just described provide all the data needed to answer the questions and ask you to use your reasoning ability to find the answers. Your best preparation for these tests, as well as for tests of facts and ideas, is to be at your physical and mental best. You, no doubt, have your own methods of getting into an exam-taking mood and keeping "in shape." The next section lists some ideas on this subject.

IV. KINDS OF QUESTIONS

Only rarely is the "essay" question, which you answer in narrative form, used in civil service tests. Civil service tests are usually of the short-answer type. Full instructions for answering these questions will be given to you at the examination. But in case this is your first experience with short-answer questions and separate answer sheets, here is what you need to know:

1) Multiple-choice Questions

Most popular of the short-answer questions is the "multiple choice" or "best answer" question. It can be used, for example, to test for factual knowledge, ability to solve problems or judgment in meeting situations found at work.

A multiple-choice question is normally one of three types—

- It can begin with an incomplete statement followed by several possible endings. You are to find the one ending which *best* completes the statement, although some of the others may not be entirely wrong.
- It can also be a complete statement in the form of a question which is answered by choosing one of the statements listed.
- It can be in the form of a problem – again you select the best answer.

Here is an example of a multiple-choice question with a discussion which should give you some clues as to the method for choosing the right answer:

When an employee has a complaint about his assignment, the action which will *best* help him overcome his difficulty is to
- A. discuss his difficulty with his coworkers
- B. take the problem to the head of the organization
- C. take the problem to the person who gave him the assignment
- D. say nothing to anyone about his complaint

In answering this question, you should study each of the choices to find which is best. Consider choice "A" – Certainly an employee may discuss his complaint with fellow employees, but no change or improvement can result, and the complaint remains unresolved. Choice "B" is a poor choice since the head of the organization probably does not know what assignment you have been given, and taking your problem to him is known as "going over the head" of the supervisor. The supervisor, or person who made the assignment, is the person who can clarify it or correct any injustice. Choice "C" is, therefore, correct. To say nothing, as in choice "D," is unwise. Supervisors have and interest in knowing the problems employees are facing, and the employee is seeking a solution to his problem.

2) True/False Questions

The "true/false" or "right/wrong" form of question is sometimes used. Here a complete statement is given. Your job is to decide whether the statement is right or wrong.

SAMPLE: A roaming cell-phone call to a nearby city costs less than a non-roaming call to a distant city.

This statement is wrong, or false, since roaming calls are more expensive.

This is not a complete list of all possible question forms, although most of the others are variations of these common types. You will always get complete directions for answering questions. Be sure you understand *how* to mark your answers – ask questions until you do.

V. RECORDING YOUR ANSWERS

Computer terminals are used more and more today for many different kinds of exams.

For an examination with very few applicants, you may be told to record your answers in the test booklet itself. Separate answer sheets are much more common. If this separate answer sheet is to be scored by machine – and this is often the case – it is highly important that you mark your answers correctly in order to get credit.

An electronic scoring machine is often used in civil service offices because of the speed with which papers can be scored. Machine-scored answer sheets must be marked with a pencil, which will be given to you. This pencil has a high graphite content which responds to the electronic scoring machine. As a matter of fact, stray dots may register as answers, so do not let your pencil rest on the answer sheet while you are pondering the correct answer. Also, if your pencil lead breaks or is otherwise defective, ask for another.

Since the answer sheet will be dropped in a slot in the scoring machine, be careful not to bend the corners or get the paper crumpled.

The answer sheet normally has five vertical columns of numbers, with 30 numbers to a column. These numbers correspond to the question numbers in your test booklet. After each number, going across the page are four or five pairs of dotted lines. These short dotted lines have small letters or numbers above them. The first two pairs may also have a "T" or "F" above the letters. This indicates that the first two pairs only are to be used if the questions are of the true-false type. If the questions are multiple choice, disregard the "T" and "F" and pay attention only to the small letters or numbers.

Answer your questions in the manner of the sample that follows:

32. The largest city in the United States is
    A. Washington, D.C.
    B. New York City
    C. Chicago
    D. Detroit
    E. San Francisco

1) Choose the answer you think is best. (New York City is the largest, so "B" is correct.)
2) Find the row of dotted lines numbered the same as the question you are answering. (Find row number 32)
3) Find the pair of dotted lines corresponding to the answer. (Find the pair of lines under the mark "B.")
4) Make a solid black mark between the dotted lines.

VI. BEFORE THE TEST

Common sense will help you find procedures to follow to get ready for an examination. Too many of us, however, overlook these sensible measures. Indeed, nervousness and fatigue have been found to be the most serious reasons why applicants fail to do their best on civil service tests. Here is a list of reminders:

- Begin your preparation early – Don't wait until the last minute to go scurrying around for books and materials or to find out what the position is all about.
- Prepare continuously – An hour a night for a week is better than an all-night cram session. This has been definitely established. What is more, a night a week for a month will return better dividends than crowding your study into a shorter period of time.
- Locate the place of the exam – You have been sent a notice telling you when and where to report for the examination. If the location is in a different town or otherwise unfamiliar to you, it would be well to inquire the best route and learn something about the building.
- Relax the night before the test – Allow your mind to rest. Do not study at all that night. Plan some mild recreation or diversion; then go to bed early and get a good night's sleep.
- Get up early enough to make a leisurely trip to the place for the test – This way unforeseen events, traffic snarls, unfamiliar buildings, etc. will not upset you.
- Dress comfortably – A written test is not a fashion show. You will be known by number and not by name, so wear something comfortable.
- Leave excess paraphernalia at home – Shopping bags and odd bundles will get in your way. You need bring only the items mentioned in the official notice you received; usually everything you need is provided. Do not bring reference books to the exam. They will only confuse those last minutes and be taken away from you when in the test room.
- Arrive somewhat ahead of time – If because of transportation schedules you must get there very early, bring a newspaper or magazine to take your mind off yourself while waiting.
- Locate the examination room – When you have found the proper room, you will be directed to the seat or part of the room where you will sit. Sometimes you are given a sheet of instructions to read while you are waiting. Do not fill out any forms until you are told to do so; just read them and be prepared.
- Relax and prepare to listen to the instructions
- If you have any physical problem that may keep you from doing your best, be sure to tell the test administrator. If you are sick or in poor health, you really cannot do your best on the exam. You can come back and take the test some other time.

VII. AT THE TEST

The day of the test is here and you have the test booklet in your hand. The temptation to get going is very strong. Caution! There is more to success than knowing the right answers. You must know how to identify your papers and understand variations in the type of short-answer question used in this particular examination. Follow these suggestions for maximum results from your efforts:

1) Cooperate with the monitor

The test administrator has a duty to create a situation in which you can be as much at ease as possible. He will give instructions, tell you when to begin, check to see that you are marking your answer sheet correctly, and so on. He is not there to guard you, although he will see that your competitors do not take unfair advantage. He wants to help you do your best.

2) Listen to all instructions

Don't jump the gun! Wait until you understand all directions. In most civil service tests you get more time than you need to answer the questions. So don't be in a hurry. Read each word of instructions until you clearly understand the meaning. Study the examples, listen to all announcements and follow directions. Ask questions if you do not understand what to do.

3) Identify your papers

Civil service exams are usually identified by number only. You will be assigned a number; you must not put your name on your test papers. Be sure to copy your number correctly. Since more than one exam may be given, copy your exact examination title.

4) Plan your time

Unless you are told that a test is a "speed" or "rate of work" test, speed itself is usually not important. Time enough to answer all the questions will be provided, but this does not mean that you have all day. An overall time limit has been set. Divide the total time (in minutes) by the number of questions to determine the approximate time you have for each question.

5) Do not linger over difficult questions

If you come across a difficult question, mark it with a paper clip (useful to have along) and come back to it when you have been through the booklet. One caution if you do this – be sure to skip a number on your answer sheet as well. Check often to be sure that you have not lost your place and that you are marking in the row numbered the same as the question you are answering.

6) Read the questions

Be sure you know what the question asks! Many capable people are unsuccessful because they failed to *read* the questions correctly.

7) Answer all questions

Unless you have been instructed that a penalty will be deducted for incorrect answers, it is better to guess than to omit a question.

8) Speed tests

It is often better NOT to guess on speed tests. It has been found that on timed tests people are tempted to spend the last few seconds before time is called in marking answers at random – without even reading them – in the hope of picking up a few extra points. To discourage this practice, the instructions may warn you that your score will be "corrected" for guessing. That is, a penalty will be applied. The incorrect answers will be deducted from the correct ones, or some other penalty formula will be used.

9) Review your answers

If you finish before time is called, go back to the questions you guessed or omitted to give them further thought. Review other answers if you have time.

10) Return your test materials

If you are ready to leave before others have finished or time is called, take ALL your materials to the monitor and leave quietly. Never take any test material with you. The monitor can discover whose papers are not complete, and taking a test booklet may be grounds for disqualification.

VIII. EXAMINATION TECHNIQUES

1) Read the general instructions carefully. These are usually printed on the first page of the exam booklet. As a rule, these instructions refer to the timing of the examination; the fact that you should not start work until the signal and must stop work at a signal, etc. If there are any *special* instructions, such as a choice of questions to be answered, make sure that you note this instruction carefully.

2) When you are ready to start work on the examination, that is as soon as the signal has been given, read the instructions to each question booklet, underline any key words or phrases, such as *least, best, outline, describe* and the like. In this way you will tend to answer as requested rather than discover on reviewing your paper that you *listed without describing*, that you selected the *worst* choice rather than the *best* choice, etc.

3) If the examination is of the objective or multiple-choice type – that is, each question will also give a series of possible answers: A, B, C or D, and you are called upon to select the best answer and write the letter next to that answer on your answer paper – it is advisable to start answering each question in turn. There may be anywhere from 50 to 100 such questions in the three or four hours allotted and you can see how much time would be taken if you read through all the questions before beginning to answer any. Furthermore, if you come across a question or group of questions which you know would be difficult to answer, it would undoubtedly affect your handling of all the other questions.

4) If the examination is of the essay type and contains but a few questions, it is a moot point as to whether you should read all the questions before starting to answer any one. Of course, if you are given a choice – say five out of seven and the like – then it is essential to read all the questions so you can eliminate the two that are most difficult. If, however, you are asked to answer all the questions, there may be danger in trying to answer the easiest one first because you may find that you will spend too much time on it. The best technique is to answer the first question, then proceed to the second, etc.

5) Time your answers. Before the exam begins, write down the time it started, then add the time allowed for the examination and write down the time it must be completed, then divide the time available somewhat as follows:

- If 3-1/2 hours are allowed, that would be 210 minutes. If you have 80 objective-type questions, that would be an average of 2-1/2 minutes per question. Allow yourself no more than 2 minutes per question, or a total of 160 minutes, which will permit about 50 minutes to review.
- If for the time allotment of 210 minutes there are 7 essay questions to answer, that would average about 30 minutes a question. Give yourself only 25 minutes per question so that you have about 35 minutes to review.

6) The most important instruction is to *read each question* and make sure you know what is wanted. The second most important instruction is to *time yourself properly* so that you answer every question. The third most important instruction is to *answer every question*. Guess if you have to but include something for each question. Remember that you will receive no credit for a blank and will probably receive some credit if you write something in answer to an essay question. If you guess a letter – say "B" for a multiple-choice question – you may have guessed right. If you leave a blank as an answer to a multiple-choice question, the examiners may respect your feelings but it will not add a point to your score. Some exams may penalize you for wrong answers, so in such cases *only*, you may not want to guess unless you have some basis for your answer.

7) Suggestions
   a. Objective-type questions
      1. Examine the question booklet for proper sequence of pages and questions
      2. Read all instructions carefully
      3. Skip any question which seems too difficult; return to it after all other questions have been answered
      4. Apportion your time properly; do not spend too much time on any single question or group of questions
      5. Note and underline key words – *all, most, fewest, least, best, worst, same, opposite,* etc.
      6. Pay particular attention to negatives
      7. Note unusual option, e.g., unduly long, short, complex, different or similar in content to the body of the question
      8. Observe the use of "hedging" words – *probably, may, most likely,* etc.
      9. Make sure that your answer is put next to the same number as the question
      10. Do not second-guess unless you have good reason to believe the second answer is definitely more correct
      11. Cross out original answer if you decide another answer is more accurate; do not erase until you are ready to hand your paper in
      12. Answer all questions; guess unless instructed otherwise
      13. Leave time for review

   b. Essay questions
      1. Read each question carefully
      2. Determine exactly what is wanted. Underline key words or phrases.
      3. Decide on outline or paragraph answer

4. Include many different points and elements unless asked to develop any one or two points or elements
5. Show impartiality by giving pros and cons unless directed to select one side only
6. Make and write down any assumptions you find necessary to answer the questions
7. Watch your English, grammar, punctuation and choice of words
8. Time your answers; don't crowd material

8) Answering the essay question

Most essay questions can be answered by framing the specific response around several key words or ideas. Here are a few such key words or ideas:

M's: manpower, materials, methods, money, management
P's: purpose, program, policy, plan, procedure, practice, problems, pitfalls, personnel, public relations
   a. Six basic steps in handling problems:
      1. Preliminary plan and background development
      2. Collect information, data and facts
      3. Analyze and interpret information, data and facts
      4. Analyze and develop solutions as well as make recommendations
      5. Prepare report and sell recommendations
      6. Install recommendations and follow up effectiveness

   b. Pitfalls to avoid
      1. *Taking things for granted* – A statement of the situation does not necessarily imply that each of the elements is necessarily true; for example, a complaint may be invalid and biased so that all that can be taken for granted is that a complaint has been registered
      2. *Considering only one side of a situation* – Wherever possible, indicate several alternatives and then point out the reasons you selected the best one
      3. *Failing to indicate follow up* – Whenever your answer indicates action on your part, make certain that you will take proper follow-up action to see how successful your recommendations, procedures or actions turn out to be
      4. *Taking too long in answering any single question* – Remember to time your answers properly

IX. AFTER THE TEST

Scoring procedures differ in detail among civil service jurisdictions although the general principles are the same. Whether the papers are hand-scored or graded by machine we have described, they are nearly always graded by number. That is, the person who marks the paper knows only the number – never the name – of the applicant. Not until all the papers have been graded will they be matched with names. If other tests, such as training and experience or oral interview ratings have been given, scores will be combined. Different parts of the examination usually have different weights. For example, the written test might count 60 percent of the final grade, and a rating of training and experience 40 percent. In many jurisdictions, veterans will have a certain number of points added to their grades.

After the final grade has been determined, the names are placed in grade order and an eligible list is established. There are various methods for resolving ties between those who get the same final grade – probably the most common is to place first the name of the person whose application was received first. Job offers are made from the eligible list in the order the names appear on it. You will be notified of your grade and your rank as soon as all these computations have been made. This will be done as rapidly as possible.

People who are found to meet the requirements in the announcement are called "eligibles." Their names are put on a list of eligible candidates. An eligible's chances of getting a job depend on how high he stands on this list and how fast agencies are filling jobs from the list.

When a job is to be filled from a list of eligibles, the agency asks for the names of people on the list of eligibles for that job. When the civil service commission receives this request, it sends to the agency the names of the three people highest on this list. Or, if the job to be filled has specialized requirements, the office sends the agency the names of the top three persons who meet these requirements from the general list.

The appointing officer makes a choice from among the three people whose names were sent to him. If the selected person accepts the appointment, the names of the others are put back on the list to be considered for future openings.

That is the rule in hiring from all kinds of eligible lists, whether they are for typist, carpenter, chemist, or something else. For every vacancy, the appointing officer has his choice of any one of the top three eligibles on the list. This explains why the person whose name is on top of the list sometimes does not get an appointment when some of the persons lower on the list do. If the appointing officer chooses the second or third eligible, the No. 1 eligible does not get a job at once, but stays on the list until he is appointed or the list is terminated.

X. HOW TO PASS THE INTERVIEW TEST

The examination for which you applied requires an oral interview test. You have already taken the written test and you are now being called for the interview test – the final part of the formal examination.

You may think that it is not possible to prepare for an interview test and that there are no procedures to follow during an interview. Our purpose is to point out some things you can do in advance that will help you and some good rules to follow and pitfalls to avoid while you are being interviewed.

What is an interview supposed to test?

The written examination is designed to test the technical knowledge and competence of the candidate; the oral is designed to evaluate intangible qualities, not readily measured otherwise, and to establish a list showing the relative fitness of each candidate – as measured against his competitors – for the position sought. Scoring is not on the basis of "right" and "wrong," but on a sliding scale of values ranging from "not passable" to "outstanding." As a matter of fact, it is possible to achieve a relatively low score without a single "incorrect" answer because of evident weakness in the qualities being measured.

Occasionally, an examination may consist entirely of an oral test – either an individual or a group oral. In such cases, information is sought concerning the technical knowledges and abilities of the candidate, since there has been no written examination for this purpose. More commonly, however, an oral test is used to supplement a written examination.

Who conducts interviews?

The composition of oral boards varies among different jurisdictions. In nearly all, a representative of the personnel department serves as chairman. One of the members of the board may be a representative of the department in which the candidate would work. In some cases, "outside experts" are used, and, frequently, a businessman or some other representative of the general public is asked to serve. Labor and management or other special groups may be represented. The aim is to secure the services of experts in the appropriate field.

However the board is composed, it is a good idea (and not at all improper or unethical) to ascertain in advance of the interview who the members are and what groups they represent. When you are introduced to them, you will have some idea of their backgrounds and interests, and at least you will not stutter and stammer over their names.

What should be done before the interview?

While knowledge about the board members is useful and takes some of the surprise element out of the interview, there is other preparation which is more substantive. It *is* possible to prepare for an oral interview – in several ways:

1) Keep a copy of your application and review it carefully before the interview

This may be the only document before the oral board, and the starting point of the interview. Know what education and experience you have listed there, and the sequence and dates of all of it. Sometimes the board will ask you to review the highlights of your experience for them; you should not have to hem and haw doing it.

2) Study the class specification and the examination announcement

Usually, the oral board has one or both of these to guide them. The qualities, characteristics or knowledges required by the position sought are stated in these documents. They offer valuable clues as to the nature of the oral interview. For example, if the job involves supervisory responsibilities, the announcement will usually indicate that knowledge of modern supervisory methods and the qualifications of the candidate as a supervisor will be tested. If so, you can expect such questions, frequently in the form of a hypothetical situation which you are expected to solve. NEVER go into an oral without knowledge of the duties and responsibilities of the job you seek.

3) Think through each qualification required

Try to visualize the kind of questions you would ask if you were a board member. How well could you answer them? Try especially to appraise your own knowledge and background in each area, *measured against the job sought*, and identify any areas in which you are weak. Be critical and realistic – do not flatter yourself.

4) Do some general reading in areas in which you feel you may be weak

For example, if the job involves supervision and your past experience has NOT, some general reading in supervisory methods and practices, particularly in the field of human relations, might be useful. Do NOT study agency procedures or detailed manuals. The oral board will be testing your understanding and capacity, not your memory.

5) Get a good night's sleep and watch your general health and mental attitude

You will want a clear head at the interview. Take care of a cold or any other minor ailment, and of course, no hangovers.

What should be done on the day of the interview?

Now comes the day of the interview itself. Give yourself plenty of time to get there. Plan to arrive somewhat ahead of the scheduled time, particularly if your appointment is in the fore part of the day. If a previous candidate fails to appear, the board might be ready for you a bit early. By early afternoon an oral board is almost invariably behind schedule if there are many candidates, and you may have to wait. Take along a book or magazine to read, or your application to review, but leave any extraneous material in the waiting room when you go in for your interview. In any event, relax and compose yourself.

The matter of dress is important. The board is forming impressions about you – from your experience, your manners, your attitude, and your appearance. Give your personal appearance careful attention. Dress your best, but not your flashiest. Choose conservative, appropriate clothing, and be sure it is immaculate. This is a business interview, and your appearance should indicate that you regard it as such. Besides, being well groomed and properly dressed will help boost your confidence.

Sooner or later, someone will call your name and escort you into the interview room. *This is it.* From here on you are on your own. It is too late for any more preparation. But remember, you asked for this opportunity to prove your fitness, and you are here because your request was granted.

What happens when you go in?

The usual sequence of events will be as follows: The clerk (who is often the board stenographer) will introduce you to the chairman of the oral board, who will introduce you to the other members of the board. Acknowledge the introductions before you sit down. Do not be surprised if you find a microphone facing you or a stenotypist sitting by. Oral interviews are usually recorded in the event of an appeal or other review.

Usually the chairman of the board will open the interview by reviewing the highlights of your education and work experience from your application – primarily for the benefit of the other members of the board, as well as to get the material into the record. Do not interrupt or comment unless there is an error or significant misinterpretation; if that is the case, do not hesitate. But do not quibble about insignificant matters. Also, he will usually ask you some question about your education, experience or your present job – partly to get you to start talking and to establish the interviewing "rapport." He may start the actual questioning, or turn it over to one of the other members. Frequently, each member undertakes the questioning on a particular area, one in which he is perhaps most competent, so you can expect each member to participate in the examination. Because time is limited, you may also expect some rather abrupt switches in the direction the questioning takes, so do not be upset by it. Normally, a board member will not pursue a single line of questioning unless he discovers a particular strength or weakness.

After each member has participated, the chairman will usually ask whether any member has any further questions, then will ask you if you have anything you wish to add. Unless you are expecting this question, it may floor you. Worse, it may start you off on an extended, extemporaneous speech. The board is not usually seeking more information. The question is principally to offer you a last opportunity to present further qualifications or to indicate that you have nothing to add. So, if you feel that a significant qualification or characteristic has been overlooked, it is proper to point it out in a sentence or so. Do not compliment the board on the thoroughness of their examination – they have been sketchy, and you know it. If you wish, merely say, "No thank you, I have nothing further to add." This is a point where you can "talk yourself out" of a good impression or fail to present an important bit of information. Remember, *you close the interview yourself.*

The chairman will then say, "That is all, Mr. _____, thank you." Do not be startled; the interview is over, and quicker than you think. Thank him, gather your belongings and take your leave. Save your sigh of relief for the other side of the door.

How to put your best foot forward

Throughout this entire process, you may feel that the board individually and collectively is trying to pierce your defenses, seek out your hidden weaknesses and embarrass and confuse you. Actually, this is not true. They are obliged to make an appraisal of your qualifications for the job you are seeking, and they want to see you in your best light. Remember, they must interview all candidates and a non-cooperative candidate may become a failure in spite of their best efforts to bring out his qualifications. Here are 15 suggestions that will help you:

1) Be natural – Keep your attitude confident, not cocky

If you are not confident that you can do the job, do not expect the board to be. Do not apologize for your weaknesses, try to bring out your strong points. The board is interested in a positive, not negative, presentation. Cockiness will antagonize any board member and make him wonder if you are covering up a weakness by a false show of strength.

2) Get comfortable, but don't lounge or sprawl

Sit erectly but not stiffly. A careless posture may lead the board to conclude that you are careless in other things, or at least that you are not impressed by the importance of the occasion. Either conclusion is natural, even if incorrect. Do not fuss with your clothing, a pencil or an ashtray. Your hands may occasionally be useful to emphasize a point; do not let them become a point of distraction.

3) Do not wisecrack or make small talk

This is a serious situation, and your attitude should show that you consider it as such. Further, the time of the board is limited – they do not want to waste it, and neither should you.

4) Do not exaggerate your experience or abilities

In the first place, from information in the application or other interviews and sources, the board may know more about you than you think. Secondly, you probably will not get away with it. An experienced board is rather adept at spotting such a situation, so do not take the chance.

5) If you know a board member, do not make a point of it, yet do not hide it

Certainly you are not fooling him, and probably not the other members of the board. Do not try to take advantage of your acquaintanceship – it will probably do you little good.

6) Do not dominate the interview

Let the board do that. They will give you the clues – do not assume that you have to do all the talking. Realize that the board has a number of questions to ask you, and do not try to take up all the interview time by showing off your extensive knowledge of the answer to the first one.

7) Be attentive

You only have 20 minutes or so, and you should keep your attention at its sharpest throughout. When a member is addressing a problem or question to you, give him your undivided attention. Address your reply principally to him, but do not exclude the other board members.

8) Do not interrupt

A board member may be stating a problem for you to analyze. He will ask you a question when the time comes. Let him state the problem, and wait for the question.

9) Make sure you understand the question

Do not try to answer until you are sure what the question is. If it is not clear, restate it in your own words or ask the board member to clarify it for you. However, do not haggle about minor elements.

10) Reply promptly but not hastily

A common entry on oral board rating sheets is "candidate responded readily," or "candidate hesitated in replies." Respond as promptly and quickly as you can, but do not jump to a hasty, ill-considered answer.

11) Do not be peremptory in your answers

A brief answer is proper – but do not fire your answer back. That is a losing game from your point of view. The board member can probably ask questions much faster than you can answer them.

12) Do not try to create the answer you think the board member wants

He is interested in what kind of mind you have and how it works – not in playing games. Furthermore, he can usually spot this practice and will actually grade you down on it.

13) Do not switch sides in your reply merely to agree with a board member

Frequently, a member will take a contrary position merely to draw you out and to see if you are willing and able to defend your point of view. Do not start a debate, yet do not surrender a good position. If a position is worth taking, it is worth defending.

14) Do not be afraid to admit an error in judgment if you are shown to be wrong

The board knows that you are forced to reply without any opportunity for careful consideration. Your answer may be demonstrably wrong. If so, admit it and get on with the interview.

15) Do not dwell at length on your present job

The opening question may relate to your present assignment. Answer the question but do not go into an extended discussion. You are being examined for a *new* job, not your present one. As a matter of fact, try to phrase ALL your answers in terms of the job for which you are being examined.

Basis of Rating

Probably you will forget most of these "do's" and "don'ts" when you walk into the oral interview room. Even remembering them all will not ensure you a passing grade. Perhaps you did not have the qualifications in the first place. But remembering them will help you to put your best foot forward, without treading on the toes of the board members.

Rumor and popular opinion to the contrary notwithstanding, an oral board wants you to make the best appearance possible. They know you are under pressure – but they also want to see how you respond to it as a guide to what your reaction would be under the pressures of the job you seek. They will be influenced by the degree of poise you display, the personal traits you show and the manner in which you respond.

ABOUT THIS BOOK

This book contains tests divided into Examination Sections. Go through each test, answering every question in the margin. At the end of each test look at the answer key and check your answers. On the ones you got wrong, look at the right answer choice and learn. Do not fill in the answers first. Do not memorize the questions and answers, but understand the answer and principles involved. On your test, the questions will likely be different from the samples. Questions are changed and new ones added. If you understand these past questions you should have success with any changes that arise. Tests may consist of several types of questions. We have additional books on each subject should more study be advisable or necessary for you. Finally, the more you study, the better prepared you will be. This book is intended to be the last thing you study before you walk into the examination room. Prior study of relevant texts is also recommended. NLC publishes some of these in our Fundamental Series. Knowledge and good sense are important factors in passing your exam. Good luck also helps. So now study this Passbook, absorb the material contained within and take that knowledge into the examination. Then do your best to pass that exam.

EXAMINATION SECTION

EXAMINATION SECTION
TEST 1

DIRECTIONS: Each question or incomplete statement is followed by several suggested answers or completions. Select the one that BEST answers the question or completes the statement. *PRINT THE LETTER OF THE CORRECT ANSWER IN THE SPACE AT THE RIGHT.*

1. Penicillin is effective in the treatment of several diseases because it   1.____
    A. builds up bodily resistance to the disease
    B. builds an immunity to the organisms causing the disease
    C. halts the growth of disease-producing organisms
    D. kills the organisms which cause the disease

2. The HIGHEST incidence of tuberculosis occurs during the ages of   2.____
    A. 1-9   B. 10-14   C. 15-30   D. 31-45

3. The MOST infectious stage of measles is the   3.____
    A. febrile   B. convalescent   C. eruptive   D. coryzal

4. When caring for a child ill with measles, you should   4.____
    A. select a room which is light and airy, but should protect the child's eyes from direct light
    B. regulate the temperature of the room to about 72-75° F
    C. keep the child in a darkened room to protect its eyes
    D. have the child wear woolen clothing for warmth

5. Ringworm on the skin is caused by a   .   5.____
    A. bacterium   B. fungus   C. protozoan   D. worm

6. Body temperature taken by rectum is _____ body temperature taken orally.   6.____
    A. 1° lower than   B. the same as
    C. 1° higher than   D. 2° higher than

7. The dishes used by a patient ill with a communicable disease should be.   7.____
    A. scraped and rinsed, then washed
    B. soaked overnight in a strong disinfectant solution
    C. boiled for twenty minutes
    D. kept separate and washed with soap and hot water

8. Cold applications tend to   8.____
    A. decrease the supply of blood in the area to which they are applied
    B. dilate the blood vessels
    C. bring a greater supply of blood to the area to which they are applied
    D. increase the pressure on the nerve endings

9. A bed cradle is a useful device for   9.____

    A. elevating an extremity
    B. keeping the weight of the upper bed covers off the patient
    C. helping to keep a restless patient in bed
    D. allowing for the free circulation of air

10. If a patient shows signs of a pressure sore at the base of the spine, the nurse should   10.____

    A. try a sitting position for the patient
    B. use small cotton rings on the pressure spot
    C. apply an ointment to the sore
    D. place an air-ring under the patient's buttocks

11. If a patient lying on her side is uncomfortable, the nurse may give her a(n)   11.____

    A. extra top cover
    B. back rest
    C. snug abdominal bandage
    D. pillow to support the lumbar region

12. The diet for a patient with gallstones MAY include   12.____

    A. grapefruit juice   B. liver
    C. cream   D. peas

13. A rich source of vitamin K is   13.____

    A. butter   B. spinach   C. oranges   D. milk

14. Flaxseed meal is prescribed for making an application of moist heat because of its   14.____

    A. medicinal properties   B. mucilaginous ingredients
    C. lightness   D. ability to retain heat

15. Of the following, the substance that is NOT commonly used as an emetic is   15.____

    A. bicarbonate of soda   B. mustard powder
    C. syrup of ipecac   D. table salt

16. Supervised practice periods are USEFUL to   16.____

    A. insure continued practice on part of students
    B. prevent wrong bonds from becoming fixed through practice
    C. supplement class instruction
    D. teach children to study

17. The science of human behavior is called   17.____

    A. psychiatry   B. mental hygiene
    C. psychology   D. psychoanalysis

18. The microscopical examination of bacteria is used to determine   18.____

    A. best conditions for growth
    B. their virulency
    C. their size, shape, etc.
    D. their relation toward certain foods

19. A disease that confers active immunity is   19.____

    A. scarlet fever   B. erysipelas
    C. pneumonia   D. common colds

20. A SERIOUS infection of the eyes is   20.____

    A. trachoma   B. myopia
    C. astigmatism   D. amblyopia

21. A substance that inhibits the growth of bacteria but does NOT destroy them is called   21.____

    A. germicide   B. disinfectant
    C. antiseptic   D. sterilizer

22. Organisms which cause diseases of the intestinal tract are   22.____

    A. colon bacillus   B. diphtheria bacillus
    C. typhoid bacillus   D. cholera spirillum

23. Proved protection has been discovered against   23.____

    A. smallpox   B. mumps
    C. common colds   D. measles

24. Strabismus is COMMONLY known as   24.____

    A. near-sightedness   B. far-sightedness
    C. cross-eyes   D. pink eyes

25. The country that has the HIGHEST death rate of mothers in childbirth is   25.____

    A. England   B. Italy   C. China   D. United States

KEY (CORRECT ANSWERS)

1.	C		11.	D
2.	C		12.	A
3.	D		13.	B
4.	A		14.	D
5.	B		15.	A
6.	C		16.	C
7.	C		17.	C
8.	A		18.	C
9.	B		19.	A
10.	D		20.	A

21.	B
22.	C
23.	A
24.	C
25.	C

TEST 2

DIRECTIONS: Each question or incomplete statement is followed by several suggested answers or completions. Select the one that BEST answers the question or completes the statement. *PRINT THE LETTER OF THE CORRECT ANSWER IN THE SPACE AT THE RIGHT.*

1. The one of the following which is NOT generally used to alleviate pain is   1.____

   A. aspirin   B. morphine   C. cocaine   D. quinine

2. The administration of a drug subcutaneously means administration by   2.____

   A. mouth
   B. injection beneath the skin
   C. application on the surface of the skin
   D. rectum

3. The one of the following which is NOT a disinfectant is   3.____

   A. boiling water   B. iodine
   C. formaldehyde   D. novocain

4. The one of the following which is LEAST related to the pulse rate of an individual is his   4.____

   A. blood pressure   B. temperature
   C. weight   D. emotional state

5. The one of the following which denotes normal vision is   5.____

   A. 20/10   B. 20/20   C. 20/30   D. 20/40

6. Of the following, the temperature which is MOST desirable for a babies' weighing room in   6.____
   a health center is

   A. 60-62° F   B. 65-68° F   C. 75-77° F   D. 85-88° F

7. Of the following, it is MOST advisable for the operator to wear dark glasses during treat-   7.____
   ments by

   A. x-ray   B. infra-red radiation
   C. diathermy   D. ultra-violet radiation

8. Of the following, the BEST method of sterilizing glassware for surgical purposes is by   8.____
   means of

   A. immersion in boiling water
   B. steaming under pressure
   C. cold sterilization
   D. washing thoroughly with soap and water

9. The apparatus used for sterilizing medical equipment by means of steam under pressure   9.____
   is the

   A. autoclave   B. manometer   C. catheter   D. reamer

10. After each use of a thermometer, it should be   10.____

    A. held under hot water for several minutes
    B. disinfected in a chemical solution
    C. rinsed in cold water
    D. wiped clean with cotton

11. The LEAST desirable action to take in administering first aid to a person suffering from   11.____
shock is to

    A. give the patient some aromatic spirits of ammonia
    B. place the patient in a reclining position and elevate his legs
    C. loosen any tight clothing and place a pillow under his head
    D. place a hot water bottle near the patient's feet

12. Of the following symptoms, the one which does NOT generally accompany a fainting   12.____
spell is

    A. a flushed face
    B. perspiration of the forehead
    C. shallow breathing
    D. a slow pulse

13. Assume that a six-year-old boy is brought to the clinic bleeding profusely from a scalp   13.____
wound. The doctor has not as yet arrived.
Of the following, the MOST effective action for you to take is to

    A. wash the wound thoroughly with soap and water to prevent infection, apply pressure on the bleeding point, then treat for shock
    B. place the boy in a comfortable position, apply tincture of iodine to the wound to prevent infection, then treat for shock
    C. give the patient a stimulant, then attempt to stop the bleeding by applying digital pressure
    D. make the boy comfortable, place a compress over the wound and bandage snugly, then treat for shock

14. Of the following, the MOST frequently used method for the diagnosis of pulmonary tuber-   14.____
culosis is the

    A. blood test   B. x-ray
    C. metabolism test   D. urinalysis

15. Of the following conditions, the one which MAY be infectious is   15.____

    A. diabetes   B. tuberculosis
    C. appendicitis   D. hypertension

16. Of the following, observation of deviations from normal body weight may aid LEAST in   16.____
determining the presence of

    A. glandular disturbances   B. malnutrition
    C. organic disturbances   D. mental deficiency

17. Leukemia is a disease of the blood characterized by a   17.____

    A. moderate increase in the red cell count and decrease in the white cell count
    B. marked decrease in the red cell count and an increase in the white cell count
    C. marked increase in the hemoglobin content
    D. marked decrease in the white cell count

18. The one of the following which is MOST commonly used in the treatment of arthritis is   18.____

    A. radium   B. an electrocardiogram
    C. a radiograph   D. diathermy

19. The fluoroscope is used CHIEFLY to   19.____

    A. provide a permanent picture of the condition of internal organs at a given time
    B. make a chart of the action of the muscles of the heart
    C. observe the internal structure and functioning of the organs of the body at a given time
    D. produce heat in the tissues of the body

20. A stethoscope is an instrument used for   20.____

    A. determining the blood pressure
    B. taking the body temperature
    C. chest examinations
    D. determining the amount of sugar in the blood

21. The Dick test is used to determine susceptibility to   21.____

    A. measles   B. scarlet fever
    C. diphtheria   D. chicken pox

22. The aorta is a(n)   22.____

    A. bone   B. artery   C. ligament   D. nerve

23. The esophagus is part of the   23.____

    A. alimentary canal   B. abdominal wall
    C. mucous membrane   D. circulatory system

24. Of the following, the one which is NOT a blood vessel is the   24.____

    A. vein   B. capillary   C. ganglion   D. artery

25. Vital statistics include data relating to   25.____

    A. births, deaths, and marriages
    B. the cost of food, clothing, and shelter
    C. the number of children per family unit
    D. diseases and their comparative mortality rates

KEY (CORRECT ANSWERS)

1.	D		11.	C
2.	B		12.	A
3.	D		13.	D
4.	C		14.	B
5.	B		15.	B
6.	C		16.	D
7.	D		17.	B
8.	B		18.	D
9.	A		19.	C
10.	B		20.	C

21.	B
22.	B
23.	A
24.	C
25.	A

TEST 3

DIRECTIONS: Each question or incomplete statement is followed by several suggested answers or completions. Select the one that BEST answers the question or completes the statement. *PRINT THE LETTER OF THE CORRECT ANSWER IN THE SPACE AT THE RIGHT.*

1. The food rich in vitamin A is   1.____

    A. liver   B. butter   C. rice   D. soy beans

2. Vitamin B promotes   2.____

    A. clear vision
    B. good digestion
    C. good dentition
    D. resistance to respiratory diseases

3. When very rapid action of a drug is desired, it is USUALLY given   3.____

    A. in pill form   B. in a capsule
    C. by hot applications   D. hypodermic injection

4. Digestion takes place MOST extensively in the   4.____

    A. mouth   B. large intestine
    C. stomach   D. small intestine

5. Faulty posture MOST frequently results from   5.____

    A. a circulatory disorder   B. anemia
    C. foot defects   D. faulty nutrition

6. The chemical substances secreted by the endocrine glands are called   6.____

    A. body builders   B. antibodies
    C. stimulants   D. hormones

7. The master or *key* gland in the body is known as the   7.____

    A. thyroid   B. adrenal   C. thymus   D. pituitary

8. Hereditary susceptibility to disease means   8.____

    A. having the germ of a disease within us at birth
    B. inheriting a disease which may later develop
    C. inheriting some physical characteristic which might be a determining factor in developing the disease
    D. congenital contraction of a specific disease

9. The DIRECT cause of local infection is   9.____

    A. lowered resistance
    B. secondary anemia
    C. introduction of pathogenic organisms
    D. a break or tear in the skin

10. Sickroom visitors should be seated   10._____

    A.   near the head of the bed out of sight of the patient but within hearing distance of the voice
    B.   at the foot of the bed where the patient may see the visitor
    C.   on a chair, at the side of the bed, within the patient's range of vision and hearing
    D.   on a chair brought near enough to the bed so that the visitor may lean comfortably on the bed to see and hear the patient without difficulty

11. The incubation period is the   11._____

    A.   time when the symptoms of illness appear
    B.   period during which the disease-producing germ is developing in the body
    C.   period during which the patient's excretions contain the disease-producing germs
    D.   period when the patient is quarantined

12. The mouth care of a bed patient is   12._____

    A.   given if the patient wants it
    B.   given as part of the daily routine
    C.   important only if the patient has a denture
    D.   important only when the patient has fever

13. A device COMMONLY used to relieve pressure on the heels and elbows is   13._____

    A.   an air cushion   B.   gauze and cotton rings
    C.   a bed cradle   D.   a folded woolen blanket

14. The Schick test is given for determining susceptibility to   14._____

    A.   scarlet fever   B.   diphtheria
    C.   smallpox   D.   measles

15. A mustard footbath is USUALLY given to relieve   15._____

    A.   convulsions
    B.   nausea
    C.   congestion in a distant area
    D.   dizziness

16. The *mode of transmission* of a communicable disease is the   16._____

    A.   medium by which the disease germ was carried to the patient
    B.   point of attack
    C.   source of the infectious agent
    D.   incubation period

17. The foods that should be stressed in the diet for the prevention of constipation are: 17._____

    A.   fruits, green vegetables, and whole grain cereals
    B.   bran, and bran-filled cereals
    C.   potatoes, meat, nuts, and white bread
    D.   soups, bread, butter, and milk

18. Body temperature taken by rectum is   18.____

    A. 1° lower than oral   B. the same as oral
    C. 1° higher than oral   D. 2° higher than oral

19. The warm mustard footbath is prepared by   19.____

    A. mixing one cup of mustard and two quarts of water and boiling same
    B. soaking feet, rubbed with musterole, in hot water
    C. dissolving prepared mustard (one cup) in three quarts of hot water
    D. adding one tablespoon of mustard previously dissolved in cool water to four quarts of warm water

20. Medications given orally may be administered in the following form: 20.____

    A. Ampule   B. Injection   C. Inunction   D. Capsule

21. The dishes used by a patient ill with a communicable disease should be   21.____

    A. scraped and rinsed, then washed
    B. soaked overnight in a strong disinfectant solution
    C. boiled for twenty minutes
    D. kept separate and washed with soap and hot water

22. The temperature taken by mouth commonly accepted as normal is   22.____

    A. 99.6° F   B. 97.6° F   C. 98.6° F   D. 96.8° F

23. The nurse should administer medicine only when   23.____

    A. the patient feels ill
    B. recommended as safe by a licensed druggist
    C. ordered by the physician
    D. the symptoms indicate the need of medication

24. The MOST important duty of the nurse is to   24.____

    A. do everything herself
    B. protect the patient from visitors
    C. have full charge of carrying out orders and nursing procedures
    D. constantly reassure the patient

25. An infectious agent is   25.____

    A. a disease
    B. the organism that causes a disease
    C. the place where the germ is found
    D. the person who carries the disease

KEY (CORRECT ANSWERS)

1.	B		11.	B
2.	B		12.	B
3.	D		13.	B
4.	D		14.	B
5.	D		15.	C
6.	D		16.	A
7.	D		17.	A
8.	C		18.	C
9.	C		19.	D
10.	C		20.	D

21.	C
22.	C
23.	C
24.	C
25.	B

TEST 4

DIRECTIONS: Each question or incomplete statement is followed by several suggested answers or completions. Select the one that BEST answers the question or completes the statement. *PRINT THE LETTER OF THE CORRECT ANSWER IN THE SPACE AT THE RIGHT.*

1. Vitamin A helps to prevent   1._____
    A. night blindness   B. beri-beri
    C. sterility   D. hemorrhage

2. When a simple enema has been ordered for the patient, the enema bag or can should be   2._____
    A. three feet above the level of the mattress
    B. six feet above the level of the mattress
    C. at a level to cause a moderate flow
    D. even with the head of the bed

3. Of the methods listed, the MOST satisfactory one for preventing the spread of the common cold is   3._____

    A. administering antitoxin
    B. administering sulpha drugs
    C. isolation of the patient
    D. avoiding crowded places

4. The germ theory of disease was formulated by   4._____
    A. Harvey   B. Roentgen   C. Pasteur   D. Trudeau

5. The stomach is located in the _____ region.   5._____
    A. epigastric   B. hypogastric
    C. right lumbar   D. umbilical

6. Good dentition is BEST promoted by   6._____

    A. adequate diet
    B. brushing the teeth after eating
    C. routine visits to the dentist
    D. a quart of milk daily

7. Bacteria thrive BEST under conditions of   7._____

    A. light, moisture, and cold
    B. sunlight, moisture, and heat
    C. heat, moisture, and a food medium
    D. darkness, cold, and dryness

8. The test to measure food energy in the body is called _____ test.   8._____
    A. mechanical ingestion   B. chemical ingestion
    C. basal metabolism   D. endocrine balance

9. The hot water bottle is a GOOD medium for the application of 　　　　　9.____

　　A. dry heat　　　　　　　　　　B. moist heat
　　C. a counter-irritant　　　　　　D. hydro-therapy

10. Cold applications tend to 　　　　　　　　　　　　　　　　　　　10.____

　　A. decrease the supply of blood in the area to which they are applied
　　B. dilate the blood vessels
　　C. bring a greater supply of blood to the area to which they are applied
　　D. increase the pressure on the nerve endings

11. An acute ear infection is MOST often caused by 　　　　　　　　　11.____

　　A. a respiratory disease　　　　B. sitting in a draft
　　C. poor nutrition　　　　　　　　D. lack of sleep

12. Red blood corpuscles which form the residue, after the serum has been removed for pro-　12.____
　　cessing, are called

　　A. gamma globulin　　　　　　　B. antigen
　　C. antitoxin　　　　　　　　　　D. plasma

13. Insulin shock therapy is COMMONLY used in the treatment of 　　　　13.____

　　A. dementia praecox　　　　　　B. malaria
　　C. neuroses　　　　　　　　　　D. diabetes

14. The test given to determine the individual's susceptibility to scarlet fever is the _____　14.____
　　test.

　　A. Dick　　　　　B. Schick　　　　　C. Mantoux　　　　D. Widal

15. Diabetes is a deficiency disease caused by the lack of an internal secretion manufac-　15.____
　　tured in the

　　A. adrenal cortex　　　　　　　B. islands of Langerhans
　　C. pineal gland　　　　　　　　D. ductless glands

16. Tuberculosis is classifed as a disease which is 　　　　　　　　　　16.____

　　A. inherited　　　　　　　　　　B. environmental
　　C. caused by diet deficiency　　D. non-communicable

17. The mineral known to be an important factor in the coagulation power of blood and the　17.____
　　control of muscle contraction is

　　A. iodine　　　　B. calcium　　　　C. phosphorus　　　D. iron

18. A carrier is a 　　　　　　　　　　　　　　　　　　　　　　　　18.____

　　A. fly or other insect which may carry a disease-producing germ
　　B. person who harbors the disease germs within his body but does not show symp-
　　　　toms of the disease
　　C. person not immune to a disease
　　D. disease-producing germ which may be carried from one person to another by
　　　　some insect

19. A famous Belgian physician who wrote a book on human anatomy was   19.____

    A. Ehrlich   B. Lister   C. Domagk   D. Vesalius

20. Hemerolopia is   20.____

    A. night blindness   B. day blindness
    C. intestinal bleeding   D. dysmenorrhea

21. A bed cradle is a USEFUL device for   21.____

    A. elevating an extremity
    B. keeping the weight of the upper bed covers off the patient
    C. helping to keep a restless patient in bed
    D. allowing for the free circulation of air

22. At the termination of a communicable disease, the patient's room should be   22.____

    A. fumigated with sulphur
    B. disinfected with lysol
    C. allowed to remain unoccupied for 48 hours
    D. scrubbed thoroughly with soap and hot water and aired

23. Three ESSENTIALS of good ventilation are   23.____

    A. no drafts, humidity low, temperature high
    B. sufficient moisture, warmth, and fresh air
    C. humidity high, temperature low, air cool
    D. air in motion, correct temperature, and humidity

24. In order to guide the mental growth and normal development of the pre-school child, we should   24.____

    A. take advantage of his readiness to learn in a secure environment
    B. tell him exactly *what* to do and *how* to do the task
    C. guide him each step of the way
    D. correct him and reward him frequently

25. The technical term for vitamin B1 is   25.____

    A. nicotinic acid   B. thiamine chloride
    C. ascorbic acid   D. niacin

KEY (CORRECT ANSWERS)

1.	A	11.	A
2.	C	12.	A
3.	C	13.	A
4.	C	14.	A
5.	A	15.	B
6.	A	16.	B
7.	C	17.	B
8.	C	18.	B
9.	A	19.	D
10.	A	20.	B

21.	B
22.	D
23.	D
24.	A
25.	B

———

EXAMINATION SECTION
TEST 1

DIRECTIONS: Each question or incomplete statement is followed by several suggested answers or completions. Select the one that BEST answers the question or completes the statement. *PRINT THE LETTER OF THE CORRECT ANSWER IN THE SPACE AT THE RIGHT.*

1. Multiphasic screening, now adopted by many health departments, is BEST defined as a   1.____

    A. new method of testing vision
    B. case finding procedure combining tests for several diseases
    C. combined vision and hearing test
    D. new method of cancer detection

2. Of the following statements that a nurse might make to a patient ill with cancer who says,   2.____
I don't think I'll ever get better. When the pain comes, I'm afraid I'll die before anyone gets here, the one which would be MOST appropriate is:

    A. I wouldn't worry about that. People do not die because of pain.
    B. Of course you'll get better. You look much better than you did the last time I was here.
    C. You should try to have someone here with you and not be alone. Then you won't be afraid.
    D. I think I understand how you feel, but why do you think you won't get better?

3. In an epidemiological study of a disease, the one of the following steps which would usu-   3.____
ally NOT be included is

    A. collecting and compiling data on the incidence, prevalence, and trends of the disease
    B. reviewing the *natural history* of the disease
    C. making a sociological study of the community in which the disease is prevalent
    D. defining gaps in knowledge and developing hypotheses on which to base further investigation

4. Adequate lighting in the school is an important part of the sight conservation program.   4.____
The school nurse familiar with standards for classroom lighting should know that the RECOMMENDED illumination on each desk for ordinary classroom work is _____ candles.

    A. 20-foot   B. 35-foot   C. 50-foot   D. 75-foot

5. The relation of fluorine to dental health has been the subject of extensive study for many   5.____
years.
Of the following statements concerning the relation of fluorine to dental caries, the one which is CORRECT is that

    A. mass medication by fluorine is now accepted as the best means of treating and curing dental caries
    B. fluoridation of water supplies, though effective, is too expensive for wide usage
    C. fluoridation is effective only in children born in areas in which fluoridation exists
    D. fluoridation prevents dental caries but does not treat or cure it

6. There are measures which are effective in the prevention of diabetes in those with an   6.____
    hereditary disposition.
    Of the following, the one which has the GREATEST value as a preventive measure is

    A. preventing acute infection
    B. preventing obesity
    C. avoidance of emotional stress
    D. avoidance of marriage with a known diabetic

7. The basis of a program of *natural childbirth* is to   7.____

    A. prevent or dispel fear through education in the physiology of pregnancy
    B. reduce premature births and the complications of pregnancy
    C. reduce the maternal and neonatal mortality rates
    D. prepare the mother's body for the muscular activity of delivery

8. The one of the following statements which is CORRECT concerning retrolental fibropla-   8.____
    sia is that it is a

    A. blood dyscrasia
    B. condition occurring in Rh negative infants whose mothers are Rh positive
    C. condition causing blindness in premature infants
    D. complication of congenital syphilis

9. Of the following factors, the one which is MOST important in maintaining optimum health   9.____
    in the older age group is

    A. regular medical supervision for early recognition and treatment of minor symptoms
    B. economic independence which gives a feeling of security
    C. avoidance of all emotional tensions
    D. adjustment of the environment to prevent physical and mental strain

10. The MOST outstanding result of antibiotic therapy in the treatment of syphilis has been to   10.____

    A. reduce the toxic effect of treatment
    B. shorten the treatment period
    C. prevent a relapse
    D. prevent late complications

11. To achieve the most effective and economical case finding for tuberculosis, mass exami-   11.____
    nations should be conducted PRIMARILY for

    A. infants under one year   B. industrial workers
    C. elementary school students   D. pre-school age group

12. Though tuberculosis occurs in all age groups, there is a certain period of life when indi-   12.____
    viduals have the greatest resistance to the infection.
    That period is

    A. under one year of age
    B. between 3 years and puberty
    C. between 15 and 35 years of age
    D. between 25 and 40 years of age

13. Drug therapy for tuberculosis has proven to be an important tool in the control of the disease in its active stage.
Of the following, the one which has had the MOST satisfactory results to date in that fewer patients develop resistance to the drug and the incidence of drug toxicity is reduced is

    13.____

    A.   para-amino-salicylic acid (P.A.S.) in combination with streptomycin
    B.   dihydro-streptomycin
    C.   streptomycin in combination with promine
    D.   penicillin

14. Studies have indicated that the use of streptomycin in the treatment of tuberculosis has GREATEST value in

    14.____

    A.   recently developed pneumonic or exudative lesions
    B.   long standing infections which have been resistant to other therapies
    C.   military T.B.
    D.   meningeal T.B.

15. The PARTICULAR effectiveness of chemotherapeutic agents in the treatment of pulmonary tuberculosis is that they

    15.____

    A.   are important adjuncts to surgery
    B.   inhibit the growth of the bacillus
    C.   heal lesions rapidly
    D.   render the patient non-infectious

KEY (CORRECT ANSWERS)

1.	B	6.	B
2.	D	7.	A
3.	C	8.	C
4.	A	9.	A
5.	D	10.	B

11.	B
12.	B
13.	A
14.	A
15.	B

TEST 2

DIRECTIONS: Each question or incomplete statement is followed by several suggested answers or completions. Select the one that BEST answers the question or completes the statement. *PRINT THE LETTER OF THE CORRECT ANSWER IN THE SPACE AT THE RIGHT.*

1. The CHIEF shortcoming of chemotherapeutic agents in the treatment of pulmonary tuberculosis is

    A.   their prohibitive cost in any long-term treatment
    B.   the toxic effects which follow their use
    C.   that their use is limited to early cases
    D.   the development of bacterial resistance by the host

1.____

2. Though precise knowledge concerning the optimum duration of chemotherapy in treating pulmonary tuberculosis is lacking, the present APPROVED practice is

    A.   continued uninterrupted treatment until the sputum is negative
    B.   short courses of treatment with rest periods in between
    C.   continued treatment for a minimum of 12 months
    D.   continued treatment for one year after a negative sputum and cultures are obtained

2.____

3. A community program for the control of tuberculosis must include school children and school personnel if it is to be a success.
    Of the following statements, the one which BEST represents expert opinion on the use of B.C.G. vaccine in the school program for tuberculosis control is that

    A.   through immunization of all school children it serves as an important control measure
    B.   its chief value is that it is an inexpensive and rapid method of case finding
    C.   it would nullify the subsequent use of the tuberculin test which is the best case finding method for schools
    D.   it is a valuable diagnostic method which would reduce the evidence of contact with active cases

3.____

4. Nutritional deficiencies are a common problem in geriatrics.
    The dietary adjustment usually necessary to maintain PROPER nutrition for the average person in the older age group is

    A.   increased proteins and vitamins
    B.   elimination of fats
    C.   increased carbohydrates
    D.   elimination of roughage

4.____

5. The death rate from cancer can be reduced by early diagnosis and treatment. It is important, therefore, for the nurse to assist in case finding.
    She should know that, of the following sites, the one which the GREATEST incidence of cancer in women occurs is the

    A.   mouth   B.   skin   C.   breast   D.   rectum

5.____

6. Many cancers appear to develop when pre-existing abnormal conditions and changes in   6.____
   the tissue are present.
   Of the following, the one which is at present considered PRECANCEROUS is

   A. fibroid tumor   B. chronic cervicitis
   C. fat tissue tumor   D. sebaceous cyst

7. The diagnosis of cancer by examination of isolated cells in body secretions is known as   7.____

   A. biopsy   B. aspiration technique
   C. histological diagnosis   D. Papanicolaou smear

8. Of the following statements concerning our present knowledge of the etiology of human   8.____
   cancer, the one which is TRUE is that

   A. there is definite evidence that some cancers are caused by a virus
   B. some types of cancer are definitely contagious
   C. there is a strong possibility that cancer is transmitted from mother to baby in utero
   D. so many factors are involved that the discovery of a single cause is unlikely

9. The National Venereal Disease Control Program carried on by the Public Health Service   9.____
   of the U.S. Government is concerned PRIMARILY with

   A. promoting medical programs to provide early effective treatment of infected individ-
      uals
   B. a national program of education in the prevention of venereal diseases
   C. distribution of free drugs to physicians for the treatment of venereal disease
   D. providing funds for the education of physicians and nurses in the treatment and
      care of venereal disease

10. Of the following, the one which is of GREATEST importance in the prevention of poliomy-   10.____
    elitis is to

    A. build up resistance with proper diet
    B. keep away from crowds during periods when the disease is prevalent
    C. immunize with gamma globulin
    D. adopt general public health measures for the protection of food and water

11. Of the following statements concerning the present status of chemotherapy in the treat-   11.____
    ment of cancer, the one which is TRUE is:

    A. Results to date indicate it may soon surpass radiation and surgery as an effective
       cure
    B. It has not proven effective except in cases where early diagnosis was made
    C. It must be used in conjunction with radiation or surgery
    D. It inhibits the growth of certain types of cancer and prolongs life but is not effective
       as a cure

12. The W.H.O. Regional Organization for Europe has set up a long-term plan for European   12.____
    health needs.
    Of the following activities, the one which is NOT planned as a major activity is

21

A. coordinating health policies in European countries
B. promoting improved service through demonstration of an ideal health program in one country
C. promoting professional and technical education for health workers in the member countries
D. providing for exchange of services among member nations

13. A health problem becomes the concern of public health authorities when the incidence is great and the mortality rate high.
In terms of this statement, of the following problems, the one which should be a PRIMARY concern is

13.____

A. venereal diseases in young adults
B. tuberculosis
C. tropical diseases among ex-servicemen and their families
D. degenerative diseases of middle and later life

14. Of the following, the one which is now considered to be the MOST common mode of transmission of poliomyelitis is

14.____

A. infected insects
B. contaminated water
C. personal contact
D. infected food

15. The incubation period for infantile paralysis is

15.____

A. usually 7 to 14 days, but may vary from 3 to 35 days
B. not known
C. one week
D. usually 48 hours, but may vary from 1 to 7 days

KEY (CORRECT ANSWERS)

1.	D		6.	B
2.	C		7.	D
3.	C		8.	D
4.	A		9.	A
5.	C		10.	B

11.	D
12.	B
13.	D
14.	C
15.	A

EXAMINATION SECTION
TEST 1

DIRECTIONS: Each question or incomplete statement is followed by several suggested answers or completions. Select the one that BEST answers the question or completes the statement. *PRINT THE LETTER OF THE CORRECT ANSWER IN THE SPACE AT THE RIGHT.*

1. A nurse arrives in a home immediately after the birth of a premature baby for whom no preparation has been made. The MOST important factor to be considered in the immediate care of the baby is

    A. maintenance of body temperature
    B. removal to a hospital
    C. feeding with breastmilk
    D. demonstration of the infant's bath to the mother
    E. securing someone to give full-time care to the baby

1.____

2. The CHIEF cause of infant mortality is

    A. gastroenteritis   B. pneumonia
    C. prematurity   D. suffocation
    E. birth injuries

2.____

3. A child who carries the RH positive factor when his mother is an RH negative may develop a condition known as

    A. hypopituitarism   B. erythroblastosis
    C. autosomal genes   D. mongolism
    E. acromegaly

3.____

4. According to studies of child development, the one of the following behavior characteristics which you would expect to find in a normal two-year-old child is

    A. bladder control day and night
    B. ability to play well with a group
    C. ability to feed himself without help
    D. ability to converse in sentences
    E. ability to ride a tricycle

4.____

5. Authorities are agreed that the BEST time to begin training a child for bladder control is

    A. as soon as the mother observes a definite rhythm in urination
    B. when the child begins to walk
    C. not until the child can indicate verbally a desire to void
    D. at one year of age
    E. at nine months of age

5.____

6. In the age group 15 to 30, the one of the following diseases which is the CHIEF cause of death is

    A. puerperal sepsis   B. heart disease
    C. tuberculosis   D. syphilis
    E. appendicitis

6.____

7. In the age group 55 to 64, the one of the following diseases which is the CHIEF cause of death is   7.____

    A.   circulatory disease   B.   pneumonia
    C.   tuberculosis   D.   hemiplegia
    E.   cancer

8. In 1976, the expectancy of life at birth had increased to about 61.5. This was a 20-year saving since 1900.   8.____
Of the following factors, the one to which MOST of this saving in life has been attributed is the

    A.   improved living conditions, as a result of higher incomes
    B.   effects of the discovery of bacteria
    C.   increase in recreational facilities which has lowered nervous tension
    D.   curtailment of arduous physical labor due to mechanical inventions
    E.   federal, state, and municipal assistance to the indigent and the handicapped

9. The term *acquired immunity,* when used in connection with communicable disease, means the   9.____

    A.   specific immunity developed as a result of a natural selection in a group of people living in any particular area
    B.   immunity existing in an area where people have never contracted the disease
    C.   immunity existing for a few months after birth given physiologically to the newborn baby by the mother
    D.   specific immunity resulting from an attack of the disease or from artificial means
    E.   immunity human beings have against certain diseases of lower animals

10. Children who have had rheumatic fever and, as a result, exhibit symptoms of heart disease, must be given special protection against   10.____

    A.   exposure to acute communicable diseases
    B.   cathartics which contain kidney irritants
    C.   dietary fads to control weight
    D.   sight and sounds which frighten them
    E.   living in an enervating warm climate

11. A twenty-one-year-old man is found by x-ray to have minimal tuberculosis. The physician orders sanitorium care. Temporarily no beds are available.   11.____
The BEST advice the nurse can give in this instance until he can be admitted to the sanitorium is to

    A.   encourage the man to visit a friend in Arizona.
    B.   plan bed rest and isolation of the patient at home where his mother can care for him
    C.   advise that he may continue work in his office position since the work is light and the lesion minimal
    D.   encourage a seashore vacation where he may lie for hours in the sun
    E.   advise an outdoor mountain vacation

12. The time of a well-prepared nurse in a busy syphilis clinic can BEST be used in   12.____

    A.   acting as receptionist to put patients at ease

    B.   giving intravenous treatments, thereby releasing the physicians to do physical
        examinations

    C.   taking histories and interpreting the disease and its treatment to patients

    D.   assisting the physician and taking notes on his physical examinations

    E.   managing the clinic smoothly so patients need not wait

13.   The effect of syphilitic involvement of the eighth nerve in individuals with congenital syph-   13.____
     ilis is that it

    A.   usually causes facial paralysis, if the patient is not treated promptly

    B.   manifests itself very slowly and, therefore, may be easily controlled

    C.   is a relatively unimportant complication of the disease and responds readily to
        treatment

    D.   may be disregarded as a probable complication of the disease if the patient is over
        6 years old

    E.   usually causes total deafness and is not readily responsive to treatment

14.   The only way in which syphilis can be detected with CERTAINTY in pregnant women is   14.____
     by

    A.   actual discovery of active lesions, since in a new case the serology will remain neg-
        ative until after parturition

    B.   a vaginal smear and dark-field examination, since in pregnancy the spirochetes
        migrate to the vagina mucosa

    C.   a careful case history, since recent discoveries indicate that serologic tests are
        non-specific in pregnancy

    D.   routine serologic tests, since the primary and secondary signs and symptoms are
        often repressed in pregnancy

    E.   the Rorschach test

15.   The method which is GENERALLY recommended for preventing premature infant deaths   15.____
     resulting from inter-cranial hemorrhage is to

    A.   administer vitamin K to the mother before delivery and to the baby after birth

    B.   give the mother massive doses of calcium by hypodermic injection

    C.   increase the amount of codliver oil given to the mother so that the calcium is better
        utilized by the baby

    D.   give the infant parathyroid hormone in order to utilize available calcium

    E.   give the baby transfusions of gum tragacanth in normal saline

16.   The MOST important factor in the control of breast cancer is   16.____

    A.   application of radium as soon as a lump appears in the breast

    B.   deep x-ray therapy of all suspected lipomas

    C.   biopsy of the glands in the axilla

    D.   operative intervention early in the disease

    E.   breastfeeding of infants as a preventive measure

17.   Although there are still many unknown factors in the complete etiology of cancer, there is   17.____
     one to which authorities agree cancer can usually be validly attributed.
     This factor is

A. the tendency to cancerous growths passed on in the chromosomes and genes
B. the mechanical action of finely divided airborne proteins
C. chronic irritation in various forms
D. degeneration of cells in the older age groups
E. the implantation, in some way yet unknown, of malignant growths

18. The type of tuberculosis that has been generalized as a result of the bacilli having been seeded into the bloodstream from a tuberculosis infection is

18.____

A. miliary tuberculosis
B. tuberculosis meningitis
C. tuberculosis enteritis
D. silicotic tuberculosis
E. tuberculosis scrofula

19. The MOST common immediate cause of unsuccessful collapse of the lung by artificial pneumothorax is

19.____

A. hemoptysis
B. cavitation
C. pleurisy with effusion
D. caseous lesion
E. pleural adhesions

20. A child is given the Mantoux test to detect the existence of tuberculosis infection. After three days, a raised edematous reddened area appears at the site of the test.
The CORRECT interpretation of the test result is:

20.____

A. A primary infection is present which makes the child completely resistant to further exogenous infections
B. The test shows evidence of infection, but does not indicate whether the process is active or quiescent
C. The test shows evidence of active pulmonary tuberculosis
D. The reaction may be due to protein sensitivity and a control test is required to eliminate this factor
E. The child has been exposed to active tuberculosis, but has not acquired an infection

21. Of the following, the one which should receive the MOST emphasis by the school nurse in order to achieve the best results in improving school health education is

21.____

A. classroom teaching in hygiene
B. home visits to expand parent education
C. assisting teachers to integrate health education in classroom teaching
D. active participation in the health education programs of Parent-Teacher Associations
E. parent education through group instruction at the time of the school health examination

22. A high school student is found to have a heart condition which warrants bed rest at home. Because only six weeks of the school term remain, the student wishes to complete the term, and is inclined to disregard the school physician's advice until the school term closes.
The BEST method the school nurse can take in handling this situation is to

22.____

A. visit the home to enlist the parents' cooperation and assist them in planning the necessary care, and encourage the student to follow the doctor's advice
B. discuss it with the school doctor and get his suggestions for adjustment in the school schedule to allow the student to complete the school term
C. refer the student to the Visiting Nurse Association for follow-up and instruction
D. advise the student that if she does remain in school to go to bed every day as soon as she gets home from school
E. advise the student to see her pharmacist for confirmation of the school physician's diagnosis

23. The one of the following criteria which is the BEST method for evaluating the success of the school health program is

A. improved health behavior as evidenced by the application of health knowledge in daily habits of living
B. an increased number of health classes in the school curriculum
C. the number of defects discovered and corrected in school children
D. the number of school children examined annually by their family physicians
E. an increased number of children entering school each year without defects

23.____

24. A kindgergarten school child is found by a visual acuity test to have 20/30 vision. The action the school nurse should take in this situation is to

A. send the child to an oculist for a complete eye examination
B. send a note to the child's parents advising that the child should wear glasses
C. do nothing since farsightedness is normal in young children
D. advise the teacher to reduce the amount of class work required of the child until the condition is corrected
E. enlist the cooperation of parents and teacher in teaching the child good eye hygiene

24.____

25. A nurse should know that blepharitis is a(n)

A. skin disease which is highly communicable
B. infection of the bladder
C. inflammation of the eyelids
D. disease caused by a fungus
E. nutritional deficiency disease

25.____

_____

KEY (CORRECT ANSWERS)

1. A	11. B
2. C	12. C
3. B	13. E
4. C	14. D
5. A	15. A
6. C	16. D
7. A	17. C
8. B	18. A
9. D	19. E
10. A	20. B

21. C
22. A
23. A
24. E
25. C

―――――

EXAMINATION SECTION
TEST 1

DIRECTIONS: Each question or incomplete statement is followed by several suggested answers or completions. Select the one that BEST answers the question or completes the statement. *PRINT THE LETTER OF THE CORRECT ANSWER IN THE SPACE AT THE RIGHT.*

1. A nurse instructing a family in the home should emphasize that of the following the MOST effective way of controlling tuberculosis infection is to

    A. soak all the patient's linen in soap and water solution for 6 hours before laundering
    B. admit no one to the room except the attendant
    C. have the patient cover his mouth and nose with disposable tissues when coughing or expectorating
    D. remove all rugs, curtains, and unnecessary furniture from the room

1.____

2. When a post-operative patient complains of pain in the calf of the leg, aggravated by dor-siflexion of the foot, the BEST course of action for the nurse to take is to recommend

    A. hot soakings
    B. walking about to relieve pain
    C. massaging locally
    D. remaining in bed and calling the doctor

2.____

3. Morbidity rates are statistics relative to

    A. births
    B. deaths
    C. sickness and disease
    D. marriages

3.____

4. The Snellen test is a

    A. visual screening test
    B. diagnostic test for syphilis
    C. blood test for anemia
    D. hearing test

4.____

5. The nurse should instruct families that the temperature of water for hot water bottles should be between

    A. 95° and 110° F
    B. 115° and 130° F
    C. 135° and 150° F
    D. 155° and 170° F

5.____

6. When planning a feeding schedule for a premature infant, it is of PRIMARY importance to

    A. feed the baby regularly every two hours
    B. establish a food tolerance since the intestinal tract is undeveloped
    C. include Vitamins A, B, C, D and K in the feeding
    D. provide for additional carbohydrates

6.____

7. B.C.G. vaccine is being given at the present time

    A. to all children with a positive tuberculin test
    B. to all children exposed to tuberculosis

7.____

    C.   to all children with minimal tuberculosis lesions
    D.   experimentally to non-reactors to the tuberculin test who are subject to frequent exposure to tuberculosis

8.   When teaching a colostomy patient self-care at home, the MOST important point for the nurse to emphasize is that   8.____

    A.   a colostomy bag is essential to assure safety from leakage
    B.   the irrigation can should hang five feet above hip level
    C.   the irrigation should be done at the same time each day
    D.   the irrigation should be followed by one hour of bed-rest

9.   The destruction of all organisms, including spores, is known as   9.____

    A.   disinfection   B.   sterilization
    C.   antiseptic action   D.   germicidal action

10.   The MOST frequent and serious complication likely to arise after a patient has under-gone surgery is   10.____

    A.   wound infection   B.   blood poisoning
    C.   respiratory infection   D.   decubitus ulcers

11.   A disarrangement of the normal relation of the bones entering into the formation of a joint BEST defines   11.____

    A.   a dislocation   B.   a fracture
    C.   a sprain   D.   ankylosis

12.   The Non-Protein Nitrogen (N.P.N.) test is a   12.____

    A.   blood test to determine renal function
    B.   blood test to determine liver function
    C.   urine test to determine concentration
    D.   patency test of the Fallopian tubes

13.   When eating pork, a person may AVOID trichinosis by   13.____

    A.   not eating it in warm weather
    B.   soaking it in salt water two hours before cooking
    C.   buying pork which has a government inspection stamp
    D.   thoroughly cooking it

14.   Beriberi is a nutritional disease caused by lack of a sufficient amount of vitamin   14.____

    A. A   B. B_1 C. B_{12} D. K

15.   The one of the following groups of foods which is the BEST source of thiamine is   15.____

    A.   milk, egg yolks, cheese, lettuce
    B.   green peas, broccoli, kale, cabbage
    C.   escarole, carrots, cream cheese
    D.   whole grain bread and cereals, pork, organ meats

16. The vitamin believed to be of GREATEST aid in the healing of wounds is vitamin   16.____

    A. B$_2$ B. B$_{12}$ C. C   D. D

17. Following the ingestion of contaminated food, acute food poisoning USUALLY occurs   17.____
after the elapse of from _____ hours.

    A. 2 to 6   B. 7 to 12
    C. 13 to 24   D. 25 to 36

18. A slowly progressive degenerative disease of the nervous system usually occurring in or   18.____
after middle life, and characterized by tremors and rigidity of the skeletal muscles, BEST
defines the condition known as

    A. arthritis   B. Parkinson's disease
    C. Jacksonian epilepsy   D. multiple sclerosis

19. Of the following, the PREFERRED site for intramuscular injections is   19.____

    A. the deltoid muscle
    B. the quadriceps muscle
    C. any section of the buttocks
    D. the upper outer quadrant of the buttock near its inner angle

20. Of the following, the one which is MALIGNANT is   20.____

    A. papilloma   B. lipoma
    C. lymphosarcoma   D. myoma

21. Of the following organisms, the one which causes MORE THAN HALF of all kidney infec-   21.____
tions is

    A. bacterium coli   B. staphylocoecus
    C. streptococcus   D. escherichia coli

22. Of the following antibiotics, the one which produces a TOXIC effect on the auditory nerve   22.____
is

    A. chloromycetin   B. aureomycin
    C. streptomycin   D. penicillin

23. Antibiotics are UNIFORMLY excreted through the   23.____

    A. skin   B. urine   C. stool   D. lungs

24. Isonicotinic acid hydrazide is used CHIEFLY in the treatment of   24.____

    A. rheumatic fever   B. arthritis
    C. cancer   D. tuberculosis

25. The one of the following which attacks the enamel of the teeth is   25.____

    A. gingivitis   B. dental caries
    C. pyorrhea alveolaris   D. vitamin C deficiency

KEY (CORRECT ANSWERS)

1.	C		11.	A
2.	D		12.	A
3.	C		13.	D
4.	A		14.	B
5.	B		15.	D
6.	B		16.	C
7.	D		17.	B
8.	C		18.	B
9.	D		19.	D
10.	C		20.	C

21.	A
22.	C
23.	B
24.	D
25.	B

TEST 2

DIRECTIONS: Each question or incomplete statement is followed by several suggested answers or completions. Select the one that BEST answers the question or completes the statement. *PRINT THE LETTER OF THE CORRECT ANSWER IN THE SPACE AT THE RIGHT.*

1. Failure of muscle coordination to bring the image of an object upon the fovea centralis retinae at the same time in each eye BEST defines the condition known as

   A. glaucoma
   B. optic neuritis
   C. retrobulbar neuritis
   D. strabismus

   1.____

2. ANOTHER term for farsightedness is

   A. hyperopia
   B. myopia
   C. ophthalmia
   D. astigmatism

   2.____

3. A condition which in its advanced stages is characterized by symptoms of halos or rainbows around light is known as

   A. cataracts
   B. detached retina
   C. glaucoma
   D. corneal ulcers

   3.____

4. Blocking of the eustachian tube in children is caused MOST often by

   A. adenoid growth around the nasal end of the tube
   B. deterioration in the inner ear
   C. ear wax
   D. perforation of the eardrum

   4.____

5. It is generally agreed among authorities that a child should have training in lip reading when successive audiometric tests indicate that the better ear shows a LOSS of _____ decibels.

   A. 5   B. 10   C. 15   D. 25

   5.____

6. The MOST satisfactory way to measure a patient for crutches is to have him

   A. stand against a wall, with his arms straight at side
   B. lie on his back, with his arms straight at side
   C. lie on his back, with his arms elevated over his head
   D. stand against a wall, with his arms extended over his head

   6.____

7. In crutch walking, the weight is placed on the

   A. quadriceps muscle
   B. trapezius muscle
   C. deltoid muscle
   D. palms of the hands with wrists in hyperextension

   7.____

8. If a nurse sees that a newborn holds his head to one side with his chin rotated in the opposite direction, she SHOULD recognize the condition as

   A. facial paralysis
   B. cerebral palsy
   C. torticollis
   D. cephalhematoma

   8.____

9. Of the following types of cerebral palsy, the one which is characterized by tense con-   9.____
   tracted muscles is

   A. spastic   B. athetoid
   C. ataxic   D. dystonic

10. Of the following communicable diseases, the one that is characterized by the eruption of   10.____
    successive crops of rose pink spots which change into vesicles and finally into crusts is

    A. chicken pox   B. German measles
    C. scarlet fever   D. measles

11. The remarkable reduction in the incidence of typhoid fever is due PRIMARILY to   11.____

    A. immunization
    B. control of human environment
    C. the use of antibiotics
    D. isolation of typhoid carriers

12. Antibodies which neutralize toxins are called   12.____

    A. lysins   B. agglutinins
    C. antitoxins   D. opsonins

13. Brucellosis is USUALLY acquired in man by   13.____

    A. direct contact with a human being having the disease
    B. direct contact with infected cattle
    C. ingestion of raw milk or milk products
    D. inhaling bacteria from the air

14. Immunity following successful vaccination against smallpox is now believed to last   14.____

    A. for the lifetime of the individual
    B. at least seven years
    C. from one to three years
    D. a varying length of time from individual to individual

15. The gamma globulin fraction of pooled human plasma is an EFFECTIVE agent for pre-   15.____
    venting or modifying

    A. chicken pox   B. measles
    C. scarlet fever   D. diphtheria

16. Of the following, the one which is capable of ALTERING the course of tuberculosis is   16.____

    A. streptomycin   B. B.C.G. vaccine
    C. the tuberculin test   D. the Schick test

17. Of the following, the FIRST symptom of spontaneous pneumothorax is   17.____

    A. tightening of the chest with or without dyspnea
    B. acute dyspnea
    C. anxious expression of the face
    D. restlessness plus anxiety

18. To function effectively in the follow-up of a venereal disease patient, the one MOST   18.____
important thing for the nurse to know is the

    A. number of contacts the patient has had
    B. correct medical diagnosis of the patient concerned
    C. structure of the family
    D. economic status of the family

19. The incubation period of neisseria gonorrhea is GENERALLY from _____ days.   19.____

    A. 3 to 6   B. 7 to 10
    C. 11 to 14   D. 15 to 18

20. Of the following, the one which prenatal syphilis SELDOM affects is the   20.____

    A. nervous system   B. spleen
    C. liver   D. heart

21. Even without treatment, a person infected with non-congenital syphilis is NOT dangerous   21.____
to others after he has had the disease _____ months.

    A. 6   B. 12   C. 18   D. 2

22. In the treatment of syphilis, the antibiotic which has proven the MOST effective, with the   22.____
LEAST toxic results, as well as the MOST economical, is

    A. streptomycin   B. aureomycin
    C. penicillin   D. chloromycetin

23. Of the following communicable diseases that may be contracted in the first trimester of   23.____
pregnancy, the one which is BELIEVED to produce malformation in the newborn is

    A. scarlet fever   B. German measles
    C. diphtheria   D. measles

24. In the normal course of pregnancy, the total blood volume   24.____

    A. decreases
    B. increases and decreases at various times
    C. remains normal
    D. increases

25. In fetal growth, the period characterized by membranous nails and tooth buds occurs at   25.____
the end of the _____ lunar month.

    A. 1st   B. 3rd   C. 5th   D. 7th

KEY (CORRECT ANSWERS)

1.	D	11.	B
2.	A	12.	C
3.	C	13.	C
4.	A	14.	D
5.	D	15.	B
6.	B	16.	A
7.	D	17.	A
8.	C	18.	B
9.	A	19.	A
10.	A	20.	D

21.	D
22.	C
23.	B
24.	D
25.	B

TEST 3

DIRECTIONS: Each question or incomplete statement is followed by several suggested answers or completions. Select the one that BEST answers the question or completes the statement. *PRINT THE LETTER OF THE CORRECT ANSWER IN THE SPACE AT THE RIGHT.*

1. The exercises included in the program of "natural childbirth" are PRIMARILY aimed at   1.____

    A. making the waiting time more interesting to the patient
    B. assuring the patient of a painless labor period
    C. relaxing the patient
    D. eliminating the use of anesthesia during labor

2. The UNDERLYING principle of "rooming in" for newborn infants and their mothers is that   2.____
    it

    A. prevents nursery infections in the baby
    B. requires less nursing time
    C. provides an opportunity for the mother to know and care for her baby while in the
        hospital
    D. encourages breast feeding

3. Erythroblastosis due to the RH factor in newborn infants MOST frequently results from   3.____

    A. transfusing an RH negative woman with RH positive blood
    B. the mating of an RH positive father and an RH negative mother
    C. the failure to determine the RH status of pregnant women
    D. transfusing the mother during pregnancy

4. A premature baby is BEST defined as an infant who   4.____

    A. is less than 9 months in gestation
    B. weighs 6 pounds at birth
    C. was born in the 7th month of gestation
    D. weighs 2500 grams or less at birth

5. Retrolental fibroplasia occurs in   5.____

    A. premature infants   B. pre-school children
    C. adolescents   D. old age

6. When advising a mother regarding infant feeding, the nurse should know that MOST   6.____
    pediatricians recommend that

    A. babies be fed when they cry
    B. mothers plan a three or four hour schedule and adhere to it without variation
    C. mothers need not adhere to a strict feeding schedule since each child has an indi-
        vidual feeding pattern which should be used as a guide
    D. infants never be fed more often than once every four hours

7. An average normal infant may FIRST be expected to sit alone at the age of _____   7.____
    months.

    A. 5   B. 7   C. 9   D. 11

8. Of the following, the GREATEST single cause of infant and neonatal mortality is   8.____

    A. accidents   B. prematurity
    C. congenital malformation   D. pneumonia

9. Of the following statements relating to epilepsy, the one which is MOST correct is that   9.____

    A. epilepsy indicates feeblemindedness
    B. children with epilepsy should be treated as invalids
    C. seizures in about 50% of children with epilepsy can best be controlled with medicines now in use
    D. children with epilepsy should have permanent home teaching

10. The MOST rapid period of biological growth is during the _____ period.   10.____

    A. prenatal   B. pre-adolescent
    C. adolescent   D. post-adolescent

11. A nurse should advise a mother that bowel training is ORDINARILY successful   11.____

    A. at the same time as bladder training
    B. earlier than bladder training
    C. later than bladder training
    D. when the child is four months old

12. When cautioning about carbon monoxide poisoning, the nurse should recommend that the family   12.____

    A. keep a fire extinguisher handy at all times
    B. inspect gas, appliances daily
    C. keep a window open at least two inches in any room where there is a gas appliance
    D. do not inspect gas appliances with wet hands

13. In the treatment of severe burns, the FIRST consideration should be given to   13.____

    A. dressing the burned area
    B. treating for shock
    C. estimating the extent of the burned area
    D. giving large amounts of fluids

14. The FIRST step recommended in first aid treatment for an animal bite is   14.____

    A. cleansing the wound thoroughly with soap under running water
    B. application of any antiseptic solution
    C. application of tincture of iodine
    D. application of tincture of iodine followed by a band-aid

Questions 15-19.

DIRECTIONS: Next to Numbers 15 through 19, write the letter preceding the disease or condition mentioned in Column II which is most closely connected with the test mentioned in Column I, Numbers 15 through 19.

Column I	Column II	
15. Aschheim-Zondek	A. tuberculosis	15. ____
16. Dick	B. syphilis	16. ____
17. Kline	C. scarlet fever	17. ____
18. Mantoux	D. pregnancy	18. ____
19. Papanicolaou	E. diphtheria	19. ____
	F. diabetes	
	G. cancer	

Questions 20-25.

DIRECTIONS: Next to Numbers 20 through 25, write the letter preceding the term mentioned in Column II which is most closely connected with the definition given in Column I, Numbers 20 through 25.

Column I	Column II	
20. Inflammation of the kidneys	A. cretinism	20. ____
21. Alzeimer's disease	B. enuresis	21. ____
22. Involuntary passage of urine	C. geriatrics	22. ____
23. White blood corpuscle	D. leucocyte	23. ____
24. A form of idiocy and dwarfism	E. nephritis	24. ____
25. Lateral curvature of the spine	F. paraphasia	25. ____
	G. scoliosis	
	H. silicosis	

_____

KEY (CORRECT ANSWERS)

1.	C	11.	B
2.	C	12.	C
3.	B	13.	B
4.	D	14.	A
5.	A	15.	D
6.	C	16.	C
7.	C	17.	B
8.	B	18.	A
9.	C	19.	G
10.	A	20.	E

21.	C
22.	B
23.	D
24.	A
25.	G

TEST 4

DIRECTIONS: Each question or incomplete statement is followed by several suggested answers or completions. Select the one that BEST answers the question or completes the statement. *PRINT THE LETTER OF THE CORRECT ANSWER IN THE SPACE AT THE RIGHT.*

1. The victim of a neck fracture should be transported   1.____

    A. face downward on a rigid support
    B. face upward on a rigid support
    C. lying on the left side of a rigid support
    D. sitting upright on a chair

2. Of the following, the PRIMARY cause of acne in adolescents is   2.____

    A. too much carbohydrate in the diet
    B. the inability of the fat gland ducts and outlets to allow passage of increased secretions of sebum
    C. lack of vitamin A in the diet
    D. lack of good personal hygiene

3. The nutritional needs of older people differ from those of young adults in that older people require MORE   3.____

    A. protein   B. minerals   C. calcium   D. calories

4. Planning for aging should be the responsibility CHIEFLY of   4.____

    A. the individual   B. the family
    C. industry   D. the total community

5. Prophylaxis against the diseases of old age is USUALLY directed toward   5.____

    A. preventing the onset of a disease
    B. preventing or minimizing the disability disease produces
    C. prohibiting all physical exercise
    D. providing for early retirement

6. Of the following, the MOST accurate statement with regard to the life expectancy of the diabetic today is that   6.____

    A. his life span is 1/3 that of the non-diabetic
    B. his life span approximates that of the non-diabetic, provided proper precautions are taken
    C. the diabetic seldom lives beyond age 60 because of complications which shorten life
    D. if diabetes occurs in childhood, the prognosis is good for a normal life span

7. N.P.H. insulin is generally considered the MOST valuable of the different types of insulin because it   7.____

    A. has a low protamine content as compared with protamine zinc insulin
    B. reaches its peak in eight hours, thus providing safety for the patient during the night

C. is well-adapted to the mild cases
D. meets the requirements of the greatest number of patients

8. When caring for elderly people with diabetes, it is MOST important for the nurse to   8.____

   A. know that all diabetics must have insulin daily
   B. understand their individual personalities and habits
   C. teach them how to do urinalysis and give their own insulin
   D. know that their diets require major adjustments

9. The GREATEST social problem affecting health which has increased in the past few   9.____
   years is

   A. juvenile delinquency
   B. juvenile narcotic addiction
   C. crowding of children in housing projects
   D. migration of industrial workers

10. The MOST important reason for the nurse to keep records of patients is to   10.____

   A. provide better service to the patients
   B. give information to other agencies in the community
   C. compile information for legal documents
   D. keep *data* for tabulating vital statistics

11. The function of the nurse on a school health council is to   11.____

   A. act in an advisory capacity to the principal and teaching staff in matters pertaining
      to health
   B. secure needed facilities for treatment of children with defects
   C. plan the health education program for the school
   D. organize the entire facilities of the school for the promotion of health

12. With regard to health services, the recommendation for enactment into law that was car-   12.____
    ried out was that

   A. the Children's Bureau be abolished
   B. compulsory health insurance be inaugurated for all people in the United States
   C. the Federal Security Agency be reorganized into a Department of Health, Educa-
      tion and Welfare
   D. the Children's Bureau and the United States Health Service be combined

13. If a nurse has been assigned the following four visits, all within a radius of a few blocks,   13.____
    she should visit FIRST the case in which a(n)

   A. anxious prenatal patient is going to be evicted from her home
   B. school child was sent home from school because of Koplik spots
   C. newborn baby is regurgitating every other feeding
   D. newborn baby was discharged against the advice of the hospital to a home in
      which the father has a positive sputum for tuberculosis

14. A nurse is assigned four visits. Of the following, the FIRST visit she should make is to a   14._____

    A. cardiac patient who receives mercuhydrin regularly twice a week
    B. patient receiving 20U. of N.P.H. insulin
    C. mother delivered of a baby by a non-nurse midwife at 4 A.M. that morning
    D. child sent home from school the previous day with a rash resembling scarlet fever

15. Assume that a mother expresses concern over her one-year-old baby's feeding habits.   15._____
As a nurse, you can BEST advise this mother by telling her that

    A. she should feed her baby, although he refuses to eat
    B. appetites of children begin to diminish at the end of the first year and continue to be small for a year or two
    C. poor eating habits in children are often a result of emotional problems between parents
    D. she should feed her child every two hours whether he is hungry or not

16. Assume that a nine-year-old boy comes to you for help. He has a splinter in his finger   16._____
which has been embedded for 24 hours and around which there is a reddened *area*.
The BEST course of action for you to take is to

    A. remove the splinter and apply an antiseptic solution
    B. wash the area with tincture of green soap, express gently, and apply an antiseptic solution
    C. have the boy soak his finger in hot water and instruct him to have his mother continue the soakings at home in order to loosen the splinter
    D. cover the area with a sterile dressing and call the mother to instruct her to take the child to a physician for treatment

17. A city of 100,000 reported 30 maternal deaths last year. Of the following, the statement   17._____
regarding the maternal death rate which is CORRECT is that it

    A. is 30%
    B. cannot be computed because we do not know the general death rate
    C. cannot be computed because we do not know the number of live births
    D. cannot be computed because we do not know the infant death rate

18. The agency which has as its objective "the attainment of the highest possible level of   18._____
health of all the people" is the

    A. American Red Cross
    B. World Health Organization
    C. United States Public Health Service
    D. The Children's Bureau

19. In the event of an atom bomb attack, civil defense authorities state that the one of the fol-   19._____
lowing which will cause the GREATEST number of deaths is

    A. radioactivity   B. injuries
    C. infections   D. hemorrhage

20. Insulin was isolated from other products of the pancreas by   20._____

    A. Louis Pasteur   B. Frederick Banting
    C. George Baker   D. Anton Von Leeuwenhoek

21. Recent studies indicate that the MOST economical and practical public health control method for dental caries is to 21.____

    A. promote a community-wide nutrition program
    B. provide community dental services for bi-yearly examination of school children
    C. provide individual daily fluoride supplements
    D. fluoridate the domestic water supply

22. During a poliomyelitis epidemic, of the following, the one precaution NOT recommended by the National Foundation for Infantile Paralysis is to 22.____

    A. keep clean
    B. avoid new groups
    C. avoid getting chilled
    D. keep children home from school

23. The LEADING cause of all deaths in the United States is 23.____

    A. cancer   B. diseases of infancy
    C. accidents   D. heart disease

24. The LEADING cause of school absences in the United States is 24.____

    A. accidents   B. skin diseases
    C. digestive disorders   D. respiratory infections

25. The National Cancer Institute established in the U.S. Public Health Service in 1937 has as its MAJOR goal 25.____

    A. research and dissemination of knowledge concerning the causes and treatment of cancer
    B. improving standards for the care of the cancer patient in both the home and hospital
    C. training of medical personnel in the treatment of cancer
    D. granting financial aid to states in the development of cancer control programs

KEY (CORRECT ANSWERS)

1.	B	11.	A
2.	B	12.	C
3.	C	13.	D
4.	D	14.	C
5.	B	15.	B
6.	B	16.	D
7.	D	17.	C
8.	B	18.	B
9.	B	19.	A
10.	A	20.	B

21.	D
22.	D
23.	D
24.	D
25.	D

EXAMINATION SECTION
TEST 1

DIRECTIONS: Each question or incomplete statement is followed by several suggested answers or completions. Select the one that BEST answers the question or completes the statement. *PRINT THE LETTER OF THE CORRECT ANSWER IN THE SPACE AT THE RIGHT.*

Questions 1-8.

DIRECTIONS: Questions 1 through 8 are to be answered on the basis of the following information

Mr. Logmarino, age 55, has been a known alcoholic for the last ten years. He was brought to the emergency room because of confusion and hemoptysis.

1. All of the following are possible diagnoses of Mr. Logmarino's condition EXCEPT   1.____

   A. cirrhosis of liver   B. ascites
   C. tuberculosis   D. esophageal varices

2. Physical examination of Mr. Logmarino is LEAST likely to reveal   2.____

   A. peripheral edema
   B. shortness of breath
   C. hypotension
   D. changes in mental status

3. Mr. Logmarino's blood test would NOT show an abnormal increase in   3.____

   A. prothrombin time   B. potassium (serum)
   C. sodium (serum)   D. blood urea nitrogen

4. How would you modify Mr. Logmarino's diet to provide adequate nutrition to him?   4.____

   A. Restrict sodium to 200-500 mg a day
   B. Restrict fluids to 1000-1500 cc a day
   C. Promote high-calorie foods and snacks
   D. All of the above

5. The MOST important measure to take to prevent edema in Mr. Logmarino is to   5.____

   A. administer diuretics
   B. restrict sodium intake
   C. administer albumin
   D. measure input and output

6. After careful diagnostic tests and physical examination, the diagnosis of cirrhosis of the liver, ascites, and esophageal varices is made.   6.____
If Mr. Logmarino begins to experience gastrointestinal bleeding, your PRIORITY should be to

   A. monitor vital signs more frequently
   B. administer fluid and blood
   C. inform the physician
   D. call the operating room for an emergency procedure

7. Mr. Logmarino had a Sengstaken-Blakemore tube inserted in an attempt to stop the bleeding. All of a sudden, he complains about respiratory difficulty. You should

    A. remove the tube immediately
    B. deflate the balloon
    C. deflate the balloon and oxygenate him
    D. remove the tube and re-intubate

7.____

8. Appropriate action was taken and the problem was discovered to have occurred due to tube dislodgement. To prevent this problem from reoccurring, you should put the patient in the _____ position.

    A. supine   B. prone
    C. upright   D. semi-Fowler's

8.____

9. The projections of renal tissue located at the tips of the renal pyramids are known as

    A. calices   B. papillae   C. cortex   D. medullae

9.____

10. A normal adult produces _____ of urine per day.

    A. 2 liters   B. 500 cc
    C. 1 liter   D. 5 liters

10.____

11. Which of the following parts of the renal tubule reabsorbs 80% of electrolytes and H_2O, all glucose, amino acids, and bicarbonate?

    A. Proximal convoluted tubule
    B. Distal convoluted tubule
    C. Loop of Henle
    D. Collecting ducts

11.____

12. The medical history, for assessment of the genitourinary system, should include any history of

    A. hypertension
    B. diabetes
    C. connective tissue diseases
    D. all of the above

12.____

13. Nursing diagnoses for the patient with a disorder of the genitourinary system may include all of the following EXCEPT

    A. sexual dysfunction
    B. alteration in comfort and fluid volume
    C. hematemesis
    D. alteration in thought processes

13.____

Questions 14-25.

DIRECTIONS: Questions 14 through 25 are to be answered on the basis of the following information.

Mr. Jackson, 55 years old, is admitted to the hospital with nausea, vomiting, diarrhea or
constipation off and on, and decreased urine output. Chronic renal failure is diagnosed.

14. All of the following are predisposing factors to chronic renal failure EXCEPT   14.____

    A.   recurrent infections
    B.   exacerbations of nephritis
    C.   hypertension
    D.   smoking

15. Diagnostic tests of Mr. Jackson's urine would be LEAST likely to show elevated   15.____

    A.   protein   B.   calcium
    C.   sodium   D.   white blood cells

16. _____ would MOST likely be decreased in Mr. Jackson's urine.   16.____

    A.   Specific gravity   B.   Sodium
    C.   Protein   D.   White blood cells

17. Pre-renal causes of renal failure include all of the following EXCEPT   17.____

    A.   decreased renal perfusion
    B.   volume expansion
    C.   congestive heart failure
    D.   altered renal hemodynamics

18. Important nursing interventions in preventing neurologic complications in patients with 18.____
    chronic renal failure include monitoring

    A.   every hour for signs of uremia
    B.   for changes in mental functioning
    C.   serum electrolytes, BUN, and creatinine as ordered
    D.   all of the above

19. All of the following are signs and symptoms of uremia EXCEPT   19.____

    A.   loss of appetite   B.   confusion
    C.   apathy   D.   hypotension

20. Nursing interventions for a patient with chronic renal failure should include   20.____

    A.   preventing neurological complications
    B.   promoting/maintaining minimal cardiovascular function
    C.   monitoring/promoting alteration in fluid and electrolyte balance
    D.   all of the above

21. To assess and maintain a patient's maximal cardiovascular function, it is IMPORTANT to 21.____

    A.   monitor blood pressure and report significant changes
    B.   auscultate for pericardial friction rib
    C.   administer diuretics as ordered and monitor output
    D.   all of the above

22. One of Mr. Jackson's kidneys is found to be polycystic, and a decision is made to remove the kidney, which is contributing to renal failure.
The preoperative care of Mr. Jackson should include all of the following EXCEPT

22.____

   A. ensuring adequate fluid intake
   B. advising patient to expect flank pain after surgery if retroperitoneal approach is used
   C. assessing electrolyte values and correcting any imbalances before surgery
   D. explaining that the patient will have a chest tube

23. Post-operative care of Mr. Jackson would NOT necessarily require

23.____

   A. assessing urine output every hour (should be 30-50 cc/hour)
   B. weighing twice a week
   C. administering analgesics as ordered
   D. encouraging early ambulation

24. Patient teaching and discharge planning for a patient with one remaining kidney should include advice regarding all of the following EXCEPT

24.____

   A. prevention of urinary stasis
   B. avoidance of activities that might cause trauma to the remaining kidney
   C. no lifting heavy objects for about 1 week
   D. need to report unexplained weight gain, decreased urine output, flank pain on unoperative site, and hematuria

25. In Mr. Jackson's condition, which of the following would be an indication for dialysis?

25.____

   A. Progressive metabolic encephalopathy
   B. Uncontrolled hyperkalemia
   C. Intractable fluid overload
   D. All of the above

KEY (CORRECT ANSWERS)

1.	C		11.	A
2.	C		12.	D
3.	B		13.	C
4.	D		14.	D
5.	B		15.	B
6.	B		16.	A
7.	C		17.	B
8.	D		18.	D
9.	B		19.	D
10.	C		20.	A

21. D
22. D
23. B
24. C
25. D

―――――――

TEST 2

DIRECTIONS: Each question or incomplete statement is followed by several suggested answers or completions. Select the one that BEST answers the question or completes the statement. *PRINT THE LETTER OF THE CORRECT ANSWER IN THE SPACE AT THE RIGHT.*

1. Bones do all of the following EXCEPT

    A. provide support to skeletal framework
    B. assist in movement by acting as levers for muscles
    C. provide site for storage of calcium only
    D. protect vital organs and soft tissues

1.____

2. It is NOT true of synovial joints that

    A. they are freely moveable joints
    B. they have a joint cavity between the articulating bone surfaces
    C. a cartilagenous capsule encloses the joint
    D. the capsule is lined with a synovial membrane

2.____

Questions 3-7.

DIRECTIONS: Questions 3 through 7 are to be answered on the basis of the following information.

Mrs. Wilson, 45 years old, is admitted to the hospital with the diagnosis of severe rheumatoid arthritis.

3. Physical examination will PROBABLY reveal

    A. painful joints
    B. muscle weakness secondary to inactivity
    C. subcutaneous nodules
    D. all of the above

3.____

4. All of the following would be included among the diagnostic test results for Mrs. Wilson EXCEPT

    A. various stages of joint disease shown by x-rays
    B. anemia
    C. elevated FSR
    D. increased white blood cells

4.____

5. Nursing interventions for Mrs. Wilson should include all of the following EXCEPT

    A. assessing joints for pain, swelling, tenderness, and limitation of motion
    B. promoting maintenance of joint mobility and muscle strength
    C. giving antibiotics
    D. promoting comfort and relief and control of pain

5.____

6. To ensure bedrest, if ordered for acute exacerbations, you should

    A. maintain proper body alignment
    B. provide a soft mattress
    C. keep joints mainly in flexion, not extension
    D. all of the above

6.____

7. On the day of discharge, you should teach Mrs. Wilson about the 　　　　　　　　7.＿＿＿＿

    A. use of prescribed medications and their side effects
    B. performance of range of motion, isometric, and prescribed exercises
    C. importance of maintaining a balance between activity and rest
    D. all of the above

Questions 8-10.

DIRECTIONS: Questions 8 through 10 are to be answered on the basis of the following information.

    Mr. Jacobs is 55 years old and has osteoarthritis.

8. All of the following are characteristics of osteoarthritis EXCEPT 　　　　　　　8.＿＿＿＿

    A. chronic nonsystemic disorder of joints
    B. women affected more than men
    C. degeneration of articular cartilage
    D. incidence increases with age

9. Nursing interventions in a patient with osteoarthritis, to prevent further trauma to joints 　　9.＿＿＿＿
   and relieve strain, should include all of the following EXCEPT

    A. encouraging rest periods throughout the day
    B. ensuring proper posture and body mechanics
    C. encouraging walking without a cane
    D. avoiding excessive weight bearing activities and continuous standing

10. You would NOT expect to find ＿＿＿＿＿ upon physical examination of Mr. Jacobs. 　　10.＿＿＿＿

    A. pain and stiffness of joints
    B. Osler's nodes
    C. Heberden's nodes
    D. decreased range of motion

Questions 11-16.

DIRECTIONS: Questions 11 through 16 are to be answered on the basis of the following information.

    Mrs. Fox, 35 years old, has been diagnosed with systemic lupus erythematosus.

11. During physical examination, the nurse should expect to find 　　　　　　　　11.＿＿＿＿

    A. butterfly rash over malar eminences
    B. alopecia
    C. oral ulcers
    D. all of the above

12. All of the following diagnostic tests may be POSITIVE in Mrs. Fox EXCEPT 　　　12.＿＿＿＿

    A. antinuclear antibody   B. C-reactive protein
    C. LE prep   D. anti-DNA antibodies

13. Hematologic abnormalities in Mrs. Fox are LEAST likely to include　　　　　　　13.____

    A. hemolytic anemia　　　　　　　　B. leukocytosis
    C. lymphopenia　　　　　　　　　　　D. thrombocytopenia

14. The LEADING cause of death in patients with systemic lupus erythematosus is　　14.____

    A. infection　　　　　　　　　　　　B. renal failure
    C. skin disease　　　　　　　　　　　D. CNS problems

15. Nursing interventions in this patient should include all of the following EXCEPT　15.____

    A. monitoring vital signs, I and O, and daily weights
    B. administering seizure medications as prophylaxis for CNS involvement
    C. assessing symptoms to determine systems involved
    D. providing psychological support to patient and family

16. Patient teaching and discharge planning for Mrs. Fox should include information con-　16.____
cerning the

    A. disease process and relationship to symptoms
    B. need to avoid physical and emotional stress
    C. need to avoid exposure to persons with infections
    D. all of the above

17. All of the following would be included in nursing intervention for a patient admitted to the　17.____
hospital with a fractured femur EXCEPT

    A. monitoring for disorientation and confusion
    B. performing neurovascular checks to the affected extremity
    C. avoiding analgesics
    D. encouraging use of trapeze to facilitate movement

18. In addition to routine care for a patient with open reduction and internal fixation, you　18.____
should

    A. check dressings for bleeding, drainage, and infection
    B. turn the patient once every day
    C. turn to the operative side only
    D. all of the above

19. All of the following measures help prevent thrombus formation EXCEPT　　　　19.____

    A. applying elastic stockings
    B. encouraging bedrest
    C. encouraging dorsiflexion of the foot
    D. administering anticoagulants as ordered

20. To prevent adduction of the affected limb and hip flexion in a patient with total hip　20.____
replacement, you should advise the patient to

    A. cross legs
    B. avoid using a raised toilet seat
    C. avoid bending down to put on shoes or socks
    D. sit in low chairs

21. The *master gland* of the body is the _____ gland.   21.____

    A. adrenal   B. thyroid
    C. pituitary   D. parathyroid

22. The anterior lobe of the pituitary gland secretes all of the following hormones EXCEPT   22.____

    A. thyroid stimulating   B. antidiuretic
    C. adrenocorticotropic   D. follicular stimulating

23. Glucagon is secreted by _____ cells of the pancreas.   23.____

    A. alpha   B. beta   C. delta   D. gamma

24. A nurse would expect to find all of the following upon physical examination of a patient   24.____
with Addison's disease EXCEPT

    A. muscle weakness
    B. bronze-like pigmentation of the skin
    C. hypertension
    D. weak pulse

25. Nursing interventions in patients with Addison's disease include   25.____

    A. administering hormone replacement therapy as ordered
    B. monitoring vital signs
    C. preventing exposure to infections
    D. all of the above

KEY (CORRECT ANSWERS)

1.	C	11.	D
2.	C	12.	B
3.	D	13.	B
4.	D	14.	A
5.	C	15.	B
6.	A	16.	D
7.	D	17.	C
8.	B	18.	A
9.	C	19.	B
10.	B	20.	C

21.	C
22.	B
23.	A
24.	C
25.	D

EXAMINATION SECTION
TEST 1

DIRECTIONS: Each question or incomplete statement is followed by several suggested answers or completions. Select the one that BEST answers the question or completes the statement. *PRINT THE LETTER OF THE CORRECT ANSWER IN THE SPACE AT THE RIGHT.*

QUESTIONS 1-8.

Mrs. Edna Fopa, 30 years old, is admitted to the hospital with a suspected incomplete abortion. She has abdominal pain and a moderate amount of vaginal bleeding.

1. Mrs. Fopa is to have a sterile vaginal examination. The licensed practical nurse who is assisting with the examination may handle the equipment by three of the following methods. Which one would be INCORRECT?

    A. Use sterile gloves
    B. Use bare hands after doing a surgical scrub
    C. Use a sterile towel
    D. Use a transfer forceps that is kept in a container of antiseptic solution

1.____

Mrs. Fopa is scheduled to have a dilatation and curettage (D and C) the next day. Her pre-operative orders include secobarbital (Seconal) at bedtime.

2. In addition to promoting sleep, Seconal is given to Mrs. Fopa to

    A. *reduce* the level of anxiety
    B. *lessen* bronchial secretions
    C. *decrease* the muscle tone of the uterus
    D. *minimize* the need for postoperative analgesia

2.____

3. When checking Mrs. Fopa's chart on the morning of surgery, the licensed practical nurse finds that there is no operative consent.
Which of these actions should the nurse take FIRST?

    A. Obtain an operative consent form and have Mrs. Fopa sign it
    B. Report the absence of an operative consent to the nurse in charge
    C. Notify the operating room staff that the operative consent has not been obtained
    D. Ask Mrs. Fopa whether she signed an operative consent form on admission to the hospital

3.____

4. Mrs. Fopa receives meperidine (Demerol) hydrochloride and atropine sulfate preoperatively.
An IMPORTANT purpose of giving atropine at this time is to

    A. increase the effect of the Demerol
    B. help prevent postoperative hemorrhaging by improving the tone of smooth muscle
    C. prevent postoperative dehydration
    D. reduce the possibility of aspiration of respiratory secretions during surgery

4.____

Mrs. Fopa has a D and C under general anesthesia. She is conscious when she is brought back to her unit.

5. As soon as Mrs. Fopa is brought back to her unit after surgery, it would be MOST impor-   5.____
tant to check her for

    A. temperature elevation   B. vaginal bleeding
    C. bladder distention   D. voluntary leg movements

6. Mrs. Fopa is instructed in perineal care.   6.____
It would be MOST important for Mrs. Fopa to give herself perineal care at which of these times?

    A. Every 4 hours for the first 24 hours postoperatively
    B. During morning and evening care
    C. After using the toilet
    D. When changing sanitary napkins

7. A red blood cell count is done for Mrs. Fopa.   7.____
Which of these ranges per cu. mm. of blood is considered to be within NORMAL limits?

    A. 7,000 to 9,000   B. 150,000 to 300,000
    C. 2,500,000 to 3,000,000   D. 4,500,000 to 5,000,000

8. An iron preparation is prescribed for Mrs. Fopa.   8.____
To reduce gastric irritation, she should take the iron preparation at which of these times?

    A. Before breakfast   B. Between meals
    C. Immediately after meals   D. At bedtime

QUESTIONS 9-18.

Viola Furry, 18 years old, is hospitalized to have a biopsy of a small growth on her right leg.

9. The physician orders that Viola's right leg be shaved and then scrubbed with an antisep-   9.____
tic solution prior to surgery. The purpose of this procedure is to

    A. sterilize the skin
    B. improve circulation to the affected area
    C. avoid contamination of the specimen
    D. reduce the possibility of infection

10. While the licensed practical nurse is preparing Viola's leg for the biopsy, Viola says, "If   10.____
this lump turns out to be cancer, what happens next?"
Which of these responses by the nurse would be MOST appropriate?

    A. "I can't say. It's really hard to know exactly what will happen"
    B. "I know you're worried. Have you spoken with your doctor about it?"
    C. "What makes you think that you might have cancer?"
    D. "It's best to wait until after the biopsy to find out if it's cancer"

The biopsy is performed and the results indicate that a malignancy is present. The physician informs Viola and her parents of the results of the biopsy. Viola is scheduled for a below-the-knee amputation of her right leg.

11. At 2 a.m. on the morning of surgery, the licensed practical nurse finds Viola awake and crying.
In addition to notifying the nurse in charge, which of these actions should the nurse take?

    A. Review with Viola the procedures that are to occur later that day
    B. Give Viola a back rub
    C. Remind Viola that she needs her sleep in preparation for the operation
    D. Encourage Viola to read a favorite magazine until she gets drowsy

11.____

12. Viola is being transferred to a stretcher to go to the operating room. Which of these illustrations shows the BEST position for the licensed practical nurse when assisting Viola in moving from the bed to the stretcher?

12.____

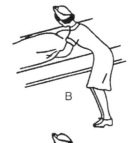
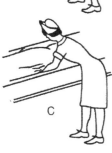

    A. A   B. B   C. C   D. D

Viola has a below-the-knee amputation of her right leg as planned. After the surgery, she is brought to the recovery room.

13. In addition to monitoring Viola's vital signs, it is ESSENTIAL to take which of these actions?

13.____

    A. Place her on her left side with pillows supporting the stump
    B. Place her on her back with sandbags on either side of the stump
    C. Check her dressing for odor
    D. Check her dressing for bleeding

Viola is transferred to the adolescent unit.

14. On Viola's second postoperative day, physical therapy is ordered for her. Two days later, she refuses her breakfast and lies in bed with her face turned toward the wall. When the licensed practical nurse who is assigned to take Viola to physical therapy goes into her room, Viola refuses to move or to acknowledge the nurse's presence.
Which of these comments would it be BEST for the nurse to make FIRST?

    A. "It's important for you to go for treatment now, Viola"
    B. "You have to stop feeling sorry for yourself if you want to get better, Viola"
    C. "Would you rather have someone else help you, Viola"
    D. "Can you tell me what's bothering you, Viola"

14.____

15. In the postoperative period, Viola's diet should be high in

    A. vitamin C and protein
    B. vitamin D and carbohydrate
    C. iron and magnesium
    D. calcium and phosphorus

15.____

16. Adjustment to the amputation is likely to be *especially* difficult for Viola because 18-year-olds characteristically

    A. have frequent mood swings
    B. have difficulty expressing their feelings verbally
    C. need to be like their peers
    D. need to be physically active

16.____

17. Viola demands a great deal of attention from the nursing staff and frequently puts her call light on to complain bitterly about her care. When the licensed practical nurse enters her room one evening to prepare her for the night, Viola says, "What the hell's going on out there? Why can't I get somebody in here?"
Which of these responses should the nurse make FIRST?

    A. "Everyone has to wait her turn, Viola. Now that I'm here, what would you like me to do"
    B. "You sound terribly unhappy, Viola. I'll be glad to do what I can to help you"
    C. "We're doing our best, Viola, but there are many patients who are really ill"
    D. "You must be more understanding, Viola. We answer your call light as quickly as we can"

17.____

18. Which of these actions should be taken if Viola experiences phantom-limb sensation?

    A. Exercise the stump
    B. Elevate the stump
    C. Divert Viola's attention
    D. Encourage Viola to talk about the feeling

18.____

QUESTIONS 19-30.

Mr. Morris Brandon, 82 years old, is admitted to the hospital with benign hypertrophy of the prostate gland. He is scheduled for a transurethral prostatectomy.

19. Where is the prostate gland located?   19.____

    A. Within the lumen of the urethra
    B. Within the seminal vesicles
    C. Around the testes
    D. Around the neck of the bladder

20. The symptoms of benign prostatic hypertrophy are usually caused by   20.____

    A. pressure of the prostate gland on other structures
    B. infiltration of the prostate gland into other tissue
    C. inflammation of the prostate gland
    D. excessive secretion from the prostate gland

21. Mr. Brandon's blood is typed and cross matched before surgery.   21.____
    A purpose of typing Mr. Brandon's blood is to

    A. determine the ratio of the formed elements in his blood to the plasma
    B. estimate the amount of blood he will need
    C. assess his bleeding pattern
    D. identify his Rh factor

22. Mr. Brandon says to the licensed practical nurse the evening before surgery, "my daugh-   22.____
ter called my minister, and he was supposed to come to see me this evening. I doubt if
he will be coming now – it's eight o'clock already."
Which of the responses would be MOST appropriate *initially*?

    A. "Would you like me to check to see if your minister is still planning to come this
       evening, Mr. Brandon"
    B. "Your minister keeps his word, Mr. Brandon. I think he'll come"
    C. "Your minister may be planning to come in the morning if he can't visit you this
       evening"
    D. "Since you feel that your minister may not come, would you like to see another min-
       ister"

Mr. Brandon has a transurethral prostatectomy. When he is returned to the unit, he has an indwelling urethral catheter that is attached to a bedside drainage container. He is to have intermittent bladder irrigations with normal saline solution. An analgesic has been ordered for him.

23. Which of these understandings should the licensed practical nurse have about the cathe-   23.____
ter irrigations for Mr. Brandon?

    A. The solution should be at room temperature and allowed to flow in by gravity
    B. No more than 50 ml. of saline should be instilled, and a moderate amount of suc-
       tion should be used to withdraw the solution
    C. The equipment and solution must be sterile, and the solution must be allowed to
       return by gravity
    D. The procedure should be continued until the returns are clear

24. If Mr. Brandon complains of pain in the bladder area, which of these measures would probably be BEST FIRST?

    24.____

    A. Finding out when he received his last medication for pain
    B. Taking his blood pressure
    C. Checking his urinary drainage apparatus
    D. Reporting his complaint to the nurse in charge

25. Three of the following measures would be appropriate in taking care of Mr. Brandon's indwelling urethral catheter.
Which one is INCORRECT?

    25.____

    A. Having the end of the drainage tubing above the level of the urine in the drainage collection container
    B. Arranging the drainage tubing so that accumulation of urine in the bladder will not occur
    C. Keeping the drainage collection container below the level of the bladder
    D. Tucking the connector on the drainage tubing under the edge of the drawsheet while the catheter is being irrigated

26. If the licensed practical nurse were to observe bright red drainage from Mr. Brandon's urethral catheter, which of these actions should be taken FIRST?

    26.____

    A. Notify the nurse in charge
    B. Elevate the foot of the bed
    C. Administer his prescribed analgesic
    D. Irrigate his bladder

27. Which of these measures will be MOST important during Mr. Brandon's morning and evening care?

    27.____

    A. Encouraging his to do his own care
    B. Giving thorough care to his perineal area
    C. Providing him with the equipment necessary for him to administer his perineal care
    D. Instructing him to maintain a high-Fowler's position during bathing

Mr. Brandon's bladder irrigations are discontinued and he is to start progressive ambulation.

28. Mr. Brandon is to get out of bed for the first time and is to ambulate.
Which of these actions should the licensed practical nurse take FIRST?

    28.____

    A. Clamp Mr. Brandon's urethral catheter
    B. Place an armchair along the side of Mr. Brandon's bed
    C. Have Mr. Brandon sit on the edge of the bed with his feet on a flat surface
    D. Provide a walker for Mr. Brandon's use

29. After Mr. Brandon's catheter is removed, which of these conditions is *most likely* to occur?

    29.____

    A. Dribbling of urine
    B. Voiding of large amount of urine
    C. Increased concentration of the urine
    D. Appearance of blood in the urine

30. Mr. Brandon says to the licensed practical nurse, "I don't have much money. Will Medicare pay the hospital bill?" The nurse's reply in order to accurately reflect current Medicare practice would be:

    A. "Medicare pays the full cost of hospitalization for all persons over 65"
    B. "Medicare is available only to those persons over 65 who are classified as financially underprivileged by the local welfare department"
    C. "Persons over 65 who are receiving Social Security benefits are eligible for Medicare benefits"
    D. "Persons over 65 who are hospitalized receive payments from Medicare automatically when hospitalization extends beyond two weeks"

30._____

KEY (CORRECT ANSWERS)

1.	B		16.	C
2.	A		17.	B
3.	B		18.	D
4.	D		19.	D
5.	B		20.	A
6.	C		21.	D
7.	D		22.	A
8.	C		23.	C
9.	D		24.	C
10.	B		25.	D
11.	B		26.	A
12.	A		27.	B
13.	D		28.	C
14.	D		29.	A
15.	A		30.	C

EXAMINATION SECTION
TEST 1

DIRECTIONS: Each question or incomplete statement is followed by several suggested answers or completions. Select the one that BEST answers the question or completes the statement. *PRINT THE LETTER OF THE CORRECT ANSWER IN THE SPACE AT THE RIGHT.*

QUESTIONS 1-6.

Mr. Francis Franco, 88 years old, has been in a skilled nursing facility for 10 months. He has generalized arteriosclerosis. Most of the patients are more than 80 years old.

1. At which of these times is disorientation *most likely* to occur in elderly people with arteriosclerotic changes in the brain?

    A. Upon arising in the morning
    B. When ambulating during the day
    C. When sitting alone in the afternoon
    D. Upon awakening during the night

1.____

2. Mr. Franco may have a diet as tolerated. The consistency of the diet served to him should be determined *primarily* by his

    A. age
    C. activity level
    B. ability to chew
    D. food preferences

2.____

3. The normal physiologic changes occurring in old age result in a DECREASED nutritional need for

    A. vitamin B complex
    C. protein
    B. calcium
    D. calories

3.____

4. It would be appropriate for the licensed practical nurse to use three of the following measures to help patients like Mr. Franco maintain normal bowel habits.
Which one is the EXCEPTION?

    A. Answering his request to go to the bathroom immediately
    B. Having him drink a glass of water before each meal
    C. Establishing a daily schedule with him for having a bowel movement
    D. Massaging his abdomen after each bowel movement

4.____

5. When the licensed practical nurse is preparing Mr. Franco for sleep, Mr. Franco says, "I wake up at night because my feet get so cold. How can I keep them warm?"
Which of these actions by the nurse would demonstrate the BEST judgment?

    A. Rub his feet briskly to improve the circulation
    B. Place a light blanket over his feet
    C. Place his feet on a covered hot-water bottle
    D. Put a covered heating pad on his feet, with the dial turned to the lowest setting

5.____

6. The GREATEST number of accidental deaths among the aged are due to   6.____

    A. falls
    B. suicide
    C. vehicular collisions
    D. unintentional ingestion of poisons

QUESTIONS 7-14.

Mr. Carlton Brooks, 44 years old, has chronic leukemia. He is admitted to the hospital with a recurrence of the symptoms of leukemia. Mr. Brooks has been told that his condition is terminal. Mr. Brooks' orders include bed rest, transfusions of whole blood, and an antiemetic p.r.n.

7. Mr. Brooks is to be given a blood transfusion in order to   7.____

    A. cause a remission of the disease and a sense of well-being
    B. depress bone marrow function and blood clotting time
    C. povide erythrocytes and hemoglobin
    D. inhibit formation of white blood cells and immune bodies

8. At the time that the blood transfusion is started, Mr. Brooks is given diphenhydramine   8.____
hydrochloride (Benadryl) intramuscularly.
The purpose of this measure is to

    A. sedate him for the treatment
    B. prevent hemolysis of the blood
    C. permit a more rapid infusion of the blood
    D. minimize a possible reaction to the blood

9. Mr. Brooks has bleeding from his gums.   9.____
The MOST probable cause of his bleeding is a(n)

    A. breakdown of red blood cells
    B. lowered platelet count
    C. overproduction of fibrinogen
    D. destruction of normal white blood cells

10. In an attempt to reduce the bleeding of Mr. Brooks' gums, the licensed practical nurse   10.____
offers him a flavored ice on a stick.
The *primary* reason for this action is that the frozen liquid

    A. keeps the mucosa moist   B. cools the mouth
    C. promotes clot formation   D. causes vasoconstriction

11. Mr. Brooks complains of nausea and eats poorly.   11.____
Which of these approaches by the licensed practical nurse would BEST promote food intake by Mr. Brooks?

    A. Serving Mr. Brooks his meals at regular mealtimes and saving uneaten food for his between-meal feedings
    B. Explaining the importance of good nutrition to Mr. Brooks and encouraging him to eat foods high in protein

C. Administering the antiemetic to Mr. Brooks a half hour before meals and offering him a diet of small, bland feedings

D. Giving the antiemetic at the time Mr. Brooks meals are served and telling him to eat what he can

12. Mr. Brooks has been depressed since the physician told him that his condition is terminal.
An IMPORTANT basic approach to the patient who is depressed is

A. responding in a mood that is similar to the patient's
B. accepting the patient's mood
C. counterbalancing the patient's mood
D. challenging the patient's mood

12.____

13. Mr. Brooks says to the licensed practical nurse, "The doctor told me that my blood condition is too severe to be treated successfully. This probably means that I don't have long to live."
Which of these responses would it be BEST for the nurse to make?

A. "Your condition is serious, Mr. Brooks"
B. "You should be thinking about making out a will, Mr. Brooks"
C. "It would be better for you to think of something else, Mr. Brooks"
D. "There is always hope, Mr. Brooks"

13.____

14. Mr. Brooks has an order for acetaminophen (Tylenol) p.r.n. For which of these reasons is Tylenol rather than aspirin given to patients who have leukemia?

A. Tylenol is more effective than aspirin in controlling the disconfort caused by this disease
B. Tylenol is absorbed in the stomach more rapidly than aspirin
C. Aspirin preparations interfere with prothrombin formation
D. Aspirin preparations have a short therapeutic effect

14.____

QUESTIONS 15-23.

Hank Bone and Bess Dresser are elderly and widowed, and are living in a residence that provides supportive services. They have several times been found in each other's rooms, engaged in necking, petting, and sexual intercourse. There is considerable gossip among residents about their behavior.

15. The sexual behavior of Mr. Bone and Mrs. Dresser is being discussed in a staff meeting.
To arrive at a plan of action, it will be MOST important to understand that they are

A. satisfying a physical instinct
B. acting rebelliously
C. meeting an emotional need
D. being exhibitionistic

15.____

16. Because Mr. Bone and Mrs. Dresser were both married before, tensions in their relation-   16.____
ship are *especially* likely to occur for which of these reasons?

    A. They may have divergent opinions on current events
    B. They are inflexible because they have lived a long time
    C. Each knows the other better as a result of having lived together in the residence
    D. Each may want the other to behave as the previous partner did

17. Mr. Bone tells the licensed practical nurse that he has two full-grown sons. He frequently   17.____
discusses with the nurse the pros and cons of the way he brought them up, and he often
wonders whether they are reasonably happy now.
The meaning of Mr. Bone's behavior is that he is

    A. living in the past
    B. attempting to be entertaining
    C. dealing with an unresolved conflict
    D. indulging in self-pity

18. In the situation described in the previous question, which of these responses would be   18.____
BEST?

    A. Indicate interest in what Mr. Bone is saying
    B. Offer to play a card game with Mr. Bone
    C. Explain to Mr. Bone that it is too late to do anything about that now
    D. Tell Mr. Bone that most fathers worry about such things

Mr. Bone has severe chest pain and is transferred to the coronary care unit in a nearby hospital.
The unit has restricted visiting hours. His orders include an electrocardiogram (EKG).

19. Which of these factors are generally considered to be related to the development of cor-   19.____
onary artery disease?

    A. Drinking moderate amounts of alcoholic beverages and participating in sports that
involve vigorous arm movements
    B. Being overweight and living under persistent pressure
    C. Having irregular meal hours and living in a climate with marked seasonal variations
    D. Eating a diet high in polyunsaturated fats and getting insufficient sleep

20. Mr. Bone's care should be based on which of these understandings about a patinet's   20.____
expected response to being admitted to a critical care unit?

    A. The complexity of the equipment in the environment will be reassuring and will
serve to lessen the patient's anxiety
    B. The sudden change in environment and the possibility of life-threatening illness will
tax the patient's usual coping mechanisms
    C. The experience will be nontraumatic if the patient has been successful in coping
with stresses in the past
    D. The competence of the staff will determine the extent of the psychological effect of
the patient's stresses

21. In preparing Mr. Bone for the EKG, the licensed practical nurse should include that he   21.____

    A. will have nothing by mouth for 12 hours before the procedure
    B. will have no discomfort during the procedure
    C. will be required to do mild exercise during the procedure
    D. must remain flat in bed for several hours after the procedure

A licensed practical nurse is with Mrs. Dresser at the residence.

22. Mrs. Dresser asks the licensed practical nurse if she can visit Mr. Bone.   22.____
    Which of these responses would be BEST?

    A. "I'll have to find out if Mr. Bone wants to see you"
    B. "I'll call Mr. Bone's unit to see if we can arrange a tine"
    C. "Mr. Bone will probably be back in a couple of days"
    D. "Mr. Bone needs rest more than anything else"

Mr. Bone's physical condition improves and he is returned to the residence. His orders include a digitalis preparation.

23. Which of these symptoms is an indication of digitalis toxicity?   23.____

    A. Thirst   B. Diuresis   C. Nausea   D. Hematuria

QUESTIONS 24-30.

Mrs. Pamela Ewing, 29 years old, is admitted to the hospital following a severe bleeding episode from a recurring peptic ulcer. Mrs. Ewing is scheduled for subtotal gastrectomy. Her orders include a cleansing enema.

24. Mrs. Ewing is to receive an enema of 1,000 ml. of solution. After receiving 100 ml. of the   24.____
    solution, Mrs. Ewing says to the licensed practical nurse, "I can't hold any more. It's going to come out!"
    Which of these actions would it be *most appropriate* for the nurse to take FIRST?

    A. Remove the rectal tube, place Mrs. Ewing on the bedpan, and then attempt to give the remainder of the fluid later if she still needs it
    B. Clamp the tubing, instruct Mrs. Ewing to take several deep breaths, and then wait a minute or two before releasing the clamp
    C. Inform Mrs. Ewing that additional fluid must be instilled and then lower the fluid container slightly
    D. Discontinue the procedure, place Mrs. Ewing on the bedpan, and then report the problem to the nurse in charge

25. On the morning of surgery, the licensed practical nurse is to care for Mrs. Ewing.   25.____
    As a basis for deciding when to give Mrs. Ewing her pre-operative medication, the nurse should understand that

    A. preoperative medication should be given prior to morning care to allow for observation of Mrs. Ewing's reaction to the medication
    B. preoperative medication should be given prior to morning care to promote optimal relaxation in Mrs. Ewing
    C. Mrs. Ewing's morning care should be completed prior to giving her preoperative medication to prevent having to disturb her
    D. Mrs. Ewing's morning care should be completed prior to giving her preoperative medication because the medication will act rapidly in a person of her age

Mrs. Ewing has a subtotal gastrectomy. She is brought to the recovery room, with a nasogastric tube in place.

26. In the immediate postoperative period, which of these assessments of Mrs. Ewing should have priority? 26.____

    A. Presence of Babinski reflex
    B. Patency of the airway
    C. Return of sensation to the legs
    D. Level of consciousness

After Mrs. Ewing reacts from anesthesia, she is brought back to her room. The nasogastric tube is attached to low, intermittent suction.

27. After Mrs. Ewing is transferred from the stretcher to her bed, the licensed practical nurse takes her vital signs. 27.____
    Which of these actions should the nurse take NEXT?

    A. Have her deep-breathe
    B. Determine her need for medication to relieve pain
    C. Check her level of consciousness
    D. Inspect her dressing

28. While Mrs. Ewing has the nasogastric tube in place, she is given mouth care frequently. 28.____
    The purpose of this measure is to

    A. maintain her ability to swallow
    B. prevent her from losing her gag reflex
    C. promote the flow of saliva
    D. stimulate peristalsis

29. While assisting Mrs. Ewing with her bath the day after her surgery, the licensed practical nurse observes that the tape on one side of her dressing is no longer adhering to her skin. Which of these actions would demonstrate the best judgment? 29.____

    A. Change the dressing
    B. Retape the dressing
    C. Use an abdominal binder to hold the dressing in place
    D. Apply tincture of benzoin to the skin under the tape and press the tape firmly against the skin

30. During the early postoperative period, Mrs. Ewing is encouraged to move her lower extremities frequently. 30.____
    The CHIEF purpose of this measure is to prevent

    A. pressure sores   B. abdominal distention
    C. muscle atrophy   D. venous stasis

KEY (CORRECT ANSWERS)

1.	D		16.	D
2.	B		17.	C
3.	D		18.	A
4.	D		19.	B
5.	B		20.	B
6.	A		21.	B
7.	C		22.	B
8.	D		23.	C
9.	B		24.	B
10.	D		25.	C
11.	C		26.	B
12.	B		27.	D
13.	A		28.	C
14.	C		29.	B
15.	C		30.	D

EXAMINATION SECTION
TEST 1

DIRECTIONS: Each question or incomplete statement is followed by several suggested answers or completions. Select the one that BEST answers the question or completes the statement. *PRINT THE LETTER OF THE CORRECT ANSWER IN THE SPACE AT THE RIGHT.*

QUESTIONS 1-7.

Mr. Robert Foreman, 59 years old, is being treated for Parkinson's disease. He is admitted to the hospital for a re-evaluation of his condition. His admission orders include diet as tolerated and activity as desired.

1. Upon Mr. Foreman's admission, which of these measures should be given priority?　　1._____

    A. Explaining to him the roles of various nursing personnel
    B. Introducing him to long-term ambulatory patients
    C. Finding out about his routines for care at home
    D. Evaluating how much he knows about his condition

2. Which of these statements about patients who have Parkinson's disease is accurate?　　2._____

    A. They have transitory memory lapses
    B. They have no intellectual impairment
    C. Their emotional lability is temporary
    D. Their mental depression cannot be overcome

3. In planning Mr. Foreman's care, GREATEST consideration should be given to　　3._____

    A. completing his care in as short a period as possible
    B. organizing his care so that he will feel unhurried
    C. encouraging him to assume full responsibility for his care
    D. providing long rest periods for him after each of his care activities

4. Mr. Foreman has been receiving levodopa (Larodopa).　　4._____
    The purpose of this medication for him is to

    A. relieve the symptoms of his disease
    B. prevent the progression of his disease
    C. promote his resistance to infection associated with his disease
    D. provide him with nutrients lost in abnormal amounts as a result of his disease

5. Mr. Foreman is to have an oil retention enema and a cleansing enema.　　5._____
    The desired effect of these measures is BEST achieved if the

    A. cleansing enema is given before the oil is instilled
    B. cleansing enema is given immediately after the oil is instilled
    C. oil is given first and remains in the bowel for a period of time before the cleansing enema is given
    D. oil and the solution for the cleansing enema are mixed thoroughly and given together

6. Mr. Foreman is to have physical therapy in preparation for discharge.   6.____
   Which of these measures can the licensed practical nurse carry out on the unit to
   assist Mr. Foreman in his rehabilitation program?

   A. Giving him warm baths with massage to relax his muscles
   B. Instructing him to use a cane to help him to walk
   C. Showing him how to do stretching exercises to loosen his joints
   D. Encouraging him to do self-care to meet his own daily needs

7. Mr. Foreman is a journalist. One day, after trying to work on a manuscript, Mr. Foreman   7.____
   suddenly sweeps the sheets of paper off the overbed table onto the floor. He exclaims
   disgustedly, "Oh, what's the use!" and starts to cry. To deal effectively with this situation,
   the licensed practical nurse should understand that

   A. complete knowledge of the effects of an illness by a patient insures acceptance of
      the illness
   B. lack of acceptance of an illness is evidenced by immature actions
   C. patients with a chronic illness tend to seek sympathy for their condition
   D. frustration occurs when patients can no longer be independent

QUESTIONS 8-11.

Miss Violene Dorisca, 22 years old, goes to a neighborhood clinic because she has a purulent
vaginal discharge. The physician suspects that Miss Dorisca has gonorrhea. She is to have a
pelvic examination.

8. The licensed practical nurse instructs Miss Dorisca to empty her bladder prior to the pel-   8.____
   vic examination.
   The CHIEF purpose of this instruction is to

   A. prevent possible rupturing of a distended bladder
   B. visualize the vaginal canal more easily
   C. aid in assessment of the pelvic organs
   D. enable the pelvic organs to reassume their normal position

The results of the diagnostic tests confirm that Miss Dorisca has gonorrhea.

9. Which of these medications is *generally* used in the treatment of gonorrhea?   9.____

   A. Penicillin   B. Streptomycin
   C. Sulfisoxazole (Gantrisin)   D. Neomycin sulfate

10. Because Miss Dorisca has gonorrhea, the information is to be reported to the Health   10.____
    Department.
    The CHIEF purpose of reporting gonorrheal infections to an official health agency is to

    A. provide for the study of current sexual habits
    B. isolate infected individuals during the treatment period
    C. identify possible infected persons
    D. compile statistics on venereal disease

11. Sterility in women that results from untreated gonorrhea is caused by   11.____

    A. scarring of the cervix
    B. cyst formation in the ovaries
    C. strictures of the fallopian tubes
    D. interference with the production of follicle-stimulating hormone (FSH)

QUESTIONS 12-23.

Bill Dupp, a 50-year-old married man, has been using nitroglycerin tablets for several months for relief of angina pectoris.

12. The pain of angina pectoris is caused by   12.____

    A. inadequate oxygen supply to the myocardium
    B. pressure on the diaphragm
    C. spasms of the intercostal muscles
    D. inefficiency of the mitral valve

13. The *desired* effect of nitroglycerin for Mr. Dupp is to   13.____

    A. constrict his peripheral blood vessels
    B. improve his coronary blood flow
    C. produce slower and stronger heartbeats
    D. increase the rate and depth of respirations

Mr. Dupp has attacks of severe chest pain that are not relieved by the nitroglycerin. He is admitted to the hospital with a myocardial infarction. Complete bed rest, oxygen by nasal cannula, oral anti-coagulant therapy, a low-sodium diet, and morphine sulfate q. 4h. p.r.n. are ordered for him.

14. Mr. Dupp has morphine one hour before the licensed practical nurse starts to give him   14.____
    morning care. When the nurse attempts to turn Mr. Dupp, he lies absolutely still, refuses to move, and holds his left shoulder with his hand.
    The MOST justifiable interpretation of this behavior is that Mr. Dupp

    A. finds this is the most comfortable position
    B. is protecting himself from his surroundings
    C. fears that the pain will recur
    D. is indicating that he is chilly

15. Some of the precautions included in Mr. Dupp's care while he is receiving oxygen are   15.____
    necessary because oxygen

    A. supports combustion
    B. increases body metabolism
    C. is toxic to the skin when administered in high concentrations
    D. is lighter than air

16. While Mr. Dupp is receiving the oral anticoagulant, it is IMPORTANT to observe him for   16.____
    evidence of

    A. hives   B. difficulty in breathing
    C. restlessness   D. hematuria

17. Which of these foods are LOWEST in sodium?   17.____

    A.   Cereals and dairy products
    B.   Bakery products and processed meats
    C.   Fresh vegetables and fruits
    D.   Canned soups and dried fruits

18. Which of these questions should be given GREATEST consideration in selecting a diver-   18.____
    sion for Mr. Dupp?

    A.   Will it be new to him?
    B.   Will it amuse him?
    C.   Does it promote relaxation?
    D.   Does it require mental concentration?

Mr. Dupp suddenly has another myocardial infarction. His condition is critical.

19. Mr. Dupp is a Roman Catholic. His wife says to the licensed practical nurse, "I want my   19.____
    husband to be anointed, but I don't want to frighten him."
    Which of these responses by the nurse would be most appropriate?

    A.   "Would you like to talk with a priest about this"
    B.   "This is a decision you must make yourself"
    C.   "Perhaps your husband isn't nearly as frightened as you are about death"
    D.   "If I were you, I wouldn't bring the matter up at this time unless your husband men-
        tions it himself"

20. Mr. Dupp's pulse is thready. A thready pulse is *accurately* described as   20.____

    A.   slow and irregular   B.   slow and forceful
    C.   rapid and weak   D.   rapid and bounding

21. To save Mr. Dupp's energy when he is acutely ill, the licensed practical nurse should *only*   21.____
    ask him questions that

    A.   are open-ended
    B.   he can answer with one word
    C.   will encourage him to understand himself
    D.   are leading

22. Mr. Dupp develops Cheyne-Stokes respirations.   22.____
    Cheyne-Stokes respirations are characterized by

    A.   stentorous, deep, labored breathing
    B.   shallow respirations, gradually increasing in rate
    C.   gradually increasing dyspnea and rapid, deep respirations
    D.   alternating periods of irregular breathing and apnea

23. Mr. Dupp dies. In the care of Mr. Dupp's body after his death, which of these measures is   23.____
    necessary?

    A.   Padding body prominences
    B.   Keeping the body in a side-lying position
    C.   Positioning the body to prevent drainage from anal and urethral orifices
    D.   Handling the body so as to protect it from disfigurement

QUESTIONS 24-30.

Mrs. Barbara Roberts, 38 years old, is admitted to the hospital with a ruptured lumbar intervertebral disc. She is placed in pelvic traction. Mrs. Roberts' orders include heat applications and meperidine (Demerol) hydorchloride p.r.n. for pain.

24. Before applying heat to Mrs. Roberts' lower back, it is essential to take which of these actions?   24.____

    A. Place a plastic protective covering on the skin before applying the source of heat
    B. Apply a thin layer of petrolatum (Vaseline) on the skin before applying the source of heat
    C. Check the temperature of the source of heat
    D. Wrap the source of heat in a towel

25. Mrs. Roberts required Demerol for pain. Before giving Mrs. Roberts the Demerol, it would be MOST important for the licensed practical nurse to take which of these actions?   25.____

    A. Check her pupillary responses
    B. Count her respirations
    C. Determine her pulse deficit
    D. Assess her urinary output

Mrs. Roberts' response to medical therapy is unsatisfactory and she is scheduled for surgery.

26. Mrs. Roberts asks the licensed practical nurse if she may put makeup on before she goes to surgery.
    Which of these responses by the nurse would be BEST?   26.____

    A. "The hospital regulations state that all makeup must be removed before you go to surgery, Mrs. Roberts"
    B. "It depends upon the amount of makeup you use, Mrs. Roberts"
    C. "Makeup will interfere with seeing any changes in the color of your skin during surgery, Mrs. Roberts"
    D. "I'll check with the nurse in charge to see if it is all right for you to put your makeup on, Mrs. Roberts"

Mrs. Roberts has a laminectomy performed under general anesthesia. After several hours in the recovery room, Mrs. Roberts is returned to her unit.

27. The logrolling technique is to be used to change Mrs. Roberts' position.
    The purpose of using this technique for her is to   27.____

    A. increase the spaces between her vertebrae
    B. provide adequate support for her extremities
    C. keep her from lying on her incision
    D. prevent strain on her surgical wound

28. Mrs. Roberts' blood pressure has been stable at 130/80, and her pulse rate has been 80. Which of these vital signs would *most clearly* indicate the development of shock?

    28.____

    A. Blood pressure 100/60; pulse 120
    B. Blood pressure 120/80; pulse 74
    C. Blood pressure 140/100; pulse 100
    D. Blood pressure 150/90; pulse 60

29. How should the licensed practical nurse assist Mrs. Roberts on to a bedpan?

    29.____

    A. Tell her to flex her knees and raise her buttocks as the bedpan is put in place
    B. Instruct her to use the overbed trapeze as a means of raising her hips so that the bedpan can be put in place
    C. Turn her onto her side, put the bedpan in place, and return her to a back-lying position on the bedpan
    D. Have her press down on the bed with her hands to raise her buttocks so that the bedpan can be put in place

30. Mrs. Roberts is ambulatory. On her fifth post-operative day, she complains of a sore area in her left calf.
How should these actions by the licensed practical nurse would be BEST?

    30.____

    A. Instruct Mrs. Roberts to remain in bed and then report the symptom to the nurse in charge
    B. Massage Mrs. Roberts' left leg gently and then take her pedal pulse
    C. Have Mrs. Roberts ambulate and then question her about the effect of the activity on her left leg
    D. Tell Mrs. Roberts to move her left leg and then palpate it for other areas of soreness

---

KEY (CORRECT ANSWERS)

1.	C	16.	D
2.	B	17.	C
3.	B	18.	C
4.	A	19.	A
5.	C	20.	C
6.	D	21.	B
7.	D	22.	D
8.	C	23.	D
9.	A	24.	C
10.	C	25.	B
11.	C	26.	C
12.	A	27.	D
13.	B	28.	A
14.	C	29.	C
15.	A	30.	A

EXAMINATION SECTION
TEST 1

DIRECTIONS: Each question or incomplete statement is followed by several suggested
answers or completions. Select the one that BEST answers the question or
completes the statement. *PRINT THE LETTER OF THE CORRECT ANSWER
IN THE SPACE AT THE RIGHT.*

QUESTIONS 1-6.

Mrs. Helen Ramirez, 51 years old, is admitted to the hospital. She has a history of ulcerative
colitis and she is scheduled to have an abdominal perineal resection.

1.   On the evening prior to surgery, the licensed practical nurse is teaching Mrs. Ramirez   1.____
coughing and breathing exercises. She says, "Stop treating me like a child. I wouldn't be
here now if I hadn't learned to breathe a long time ago."
Which of these responses should the nurse make?

   A.   "You know the reason for doing this"
   B.   "You feel I'm talking down to you"
   C.   "You're overreacting"
   D.   "No one else has had that complaint"

2.   On the morning of her surgery, Mrs. Ramirez has a nasogastric tube inserted. The pur-   2.____
pose of this tube for Mrs. Ramirez is to

   A.   remove gas and fluids from the stomach
   B.   promote peristalsis in the large intestine
   C.   prevent accumulation of fecal matter in the large intestine
   D.   provide a means of administering nourishment postoperatively

Mrs. Ramirez has surgery as scheduled and an ileostomy is performed. She has an ileostomy
bag in place. Her condition is good when she is returned to the unit.

3.   In Mrs. Ramirez's early postoperative care, it would be MOST important to take mea-   3.____
sures to

   A.   improve her respiratory function
   B.   increase her nutritional intake
   C.   establish a routine pattern for urine elimination
   D.   promote expulsion of flatus

4.   When changing Mrs. Ramirez's ileostomy bag, it is especially important that the licensed   4.____
practical nurse

   A.   refrain from showing distaste
   B.   maintain strict surgical asepsis
   C.   explain the details of the procedure
   D.   wipe the stoma with a mild antiseptic

5. Arrangements are made for Mrs. Ramirez to be visited by a woman who has adjusted well to her ileostomy.
   Which of these actions by the licensed practical nurse would *probably* promote the effectiveness of the visit?

   A. Remain in the room while the interview is in progress
   B. Return to the room periodically to answer any questions that may arise
   C. Provide a quiet, private setting for the visit
   D. Maintain a detached manner until the visit is over

   5.____

6. On several occasions, Mrs. Ramirez is observed picking at the food on her tray and eating very little. When questioned by the licensed practical nurse, Mrs. Ramirez says that she doesn't feel like eating.
   Which of these actions by the nurse would be BEST?

   A. Ask Mrs. Ramirez if she would like her husband to bring in food from home
   B. Explain to Mrs. Ramirez the importance of good nutrition to her recovery
   C. Tell Mrs. Ramirez that her refusal to eat will have to be reported to both the nurse in charge and the physician
   D. Find out if Mrs. Ramirez likes the meals she has been served

   6.____

QUESTIONS 7-18.

Mrs. Betty Lou Chesterfield, 45 years old, is admitted to the surgical unit. She is scheduled to have a bronchoscopy. Cancer of the lung is suspected.

7. Following the bronchoscopy, it is ESSENTIAL that Mrs. Chesterfield receive which of these instructions?

   A. "Call the nurse before you take a drink of anything"
   B. "Take deep breaths and cough every hour"
   C. "Tell us whenever you wish to get out of bed"
   D. "Avoid talking for three hours"

   7.____

8. Which of these symptoms experienced by a patient who has just had a bronchoscopy would be most indicative of a serious complication of the procedure.

   A. Coughing   B. Difficulty in breathing
   C. Hoarseness   D. Pain when swallowing

   8.____

The results of Mrs. Chesterfield's diagnostic tests indicate that she has cancer of the lung. A lobectomy of her right lung is scheduled and she is informed of her prognosis.

9. Mrs. Chesterfield expresses discouragement about her diagnosis and her surgery.
   Which of these measures by the licensed practical nurse would *probably* provide the MOST emotional support for Mrs. Chesterfield?

   A. Talking to her
   B. Encouraging her family to visit
   C. Trying to change her mood
   D. Listening to her attentively

   9.____

10. Mrs. Chesterfield will have a chest tube attached to underwater drainage following her surgery.
The *primary* purpose of the chest tube is to

    10._____

    A. allow for the removal of fluid and air
    B. make deep breathing and coughing easier
    C. prevent rapid re-expansion of the lung
    D. control pulmonary hemorrhage

Mrs. Chesterfield has a lobectomy of her right lung. Following a stay in the recovery room, she is brought back to her unit with a chest tube in place. Mrs. Chesterfield's orders include morphine sulfate q. 4h. p.r.n., oxygen by nasal cannula, and diet as tolerated.

11. Mrs. Chesterfield's chest tube is attached to a glass tube that extends below the level of the fluid in her chest drainage receptacle. The fluid in the glass tube rises when Mrs. Chesterfield inhales and falls when she exhales. Which of these interpretations of this finding is accurate?

    11._____

    A. Oxygen is being lost through Mrs. Chesterfield's chest tube
    B. There is an air leak within the drainage system
    C. The apparatus is functioning properly
    D. Air is being drawn into Mrs. Chesterfield's chest cavity

12. Before oxygen is administered to Mrs. Chesterfield, it should be humidified in order to

    12._____

    A. *decrease* the concentration of oxygen during respiration
    B. prevent the oxygen from drying the mucous membranes of the respiratory tract
    C. *reduce* the pressure of the oxygen to normal before inhalation
    D. let the water particles carry the dissolved oxygen to the alveoli

13. While Mrs. Chesterfield is receiving oxygen, three of the following measures may be carried out for her. Which one is CONTRAINDICATED?

    13._____

    A. Taking her temperature orally
    B. Giving her sponge baths
    C. Urging her to drink fluids
    D. Assisting her to deep-breathe and cough

14. All of the following beverages are available for evening nourishment on Mrs. Chesterfield's unit.
Assuming that servings are average, which of these drinks would provide the GREATEST amount of a vitamin that promotes healing?

    14._____

    A. Tea with lemon   B. Apple juice
    C. Tomato juice   D. Prune juice

15. During the evening of the second post-operative day, Mrs. Chesterfield complains of pain.
Which of these actions should the licensed practical nurse take FIRST?

    15._____

    A. Check her chart to ascertain the time of her last dose of medication for pain
    B. Report her symptoms to the medication nurse
    C. Give her a soothing back rub and change her linen
    D. Ask her to describe her pain

On Mrs. Chesterfield's third postoperative day, her temperature begins to rise above the normal level. The physician's orders include a tepid water sponge bath for Mrs. Chesterfield if her temperature should rise above 102° F. (38.9° C). At 8 p.m., the licensed practical nurse takes Mrs. Chesterfield's temperature. It is 103° F. (39.4° C).

16. Body heat is lost through the use of a tepid water sponge bath by　　　　16.＿＿＿＿

    A. production of more perspiration
    B. stimulation of the cold receptor endings in the skin
    C. penetration of water into the pores to cool the underlying tissues
    D. evaporation of water from the skin

17. On which of these area of Mrs. Chesterfield's body should the licensed practical nurse　　17.＿＿＿＿
place cool, moist cloths during the tepid water sponge bath?

    A. Groin and axillae
    B. Back and neck
    C. Upper and lower extremities
    D. Feet and head

18. Mrs. Chesterfield is to have increased fluids, but she is reluctant to drink.　　18.＿＿＿＿
Which of these measures will probably help MOST to increase her fluid intake?

    A. Explaining to her that she will need fluid until her infection has cleared up
    B. Offering her a small glass of fluid every hour
    C. Serving her sweetened liquids between meals
    D. Keeping a pitcher of water on her bedside table

QUESTIONS 19-24.

Mr. John Brook, 22 years old, is brought to the emergency room following a motorcycle accident. He has a head injury and is semicomatose.

19. When Mr. Brook arrives in the emergency room, the INITIAL action that should be taken　19.＿＿＿＿
is to

    A. check his vital signs
    B. assess the extent of his injury
    C. determine the patency of his airway
    D. institute measures to prevent infection

Mr. Brook is admitted to the hospital. His orders include a spinal tap.

20. When Mr. Brook is brought to the unit, he should be placed in which of these positions?　20.＿＿＿＿

    A. Head elevated slightly and turned to the side
    B. Supine, with hyperextension of the neck
    C. Legs elevated and head on a small, firm pillow
    D. Trendelenburg

21. During the spinal tap, the *primary* function of the licensed practical nurse is to   21._____

    A. explain to the patient the steps of the procedure as they occur
    B. help the patient to remain motionless
    C. prepare the labels for the fluid specimens
    D. apply pressure to the insertion site as the needle is being removed

22. One morning when the licensed practical nurse enters Mr. Brook's room, he is beginning   22._____
to have a seizure.
Which of these actions should the nurse take?

    A. Suction his oropharynx
    B. Restrain his extremities
    C. Help him to turn onto his abdomen
    D. Observe the progress of his tremors

23. It will be important to make three of the following observations of Mr. Brook while he is   23._____
having the seizure. The one that would be UNNECESSARY is of the

    A. rate and volume of his pulse
    B. presence or absence of incontinence
    C. length of his seizure
    D. parts of his body affected by the seizure

24. The early onset of increased intracranial pressure would be indicated by which of these   24._____
signs?

    A. Oliguria
    B. Pallor
    C. Widening pulse pressure
    D. Sudden decrease in body temperature

QUESTIONS 25-30.

Mr. Digger Barnes, 63 years old, is admitted to the hospital for observation following a car accident. The next day, it is determined that he has no physical injury resulting from the accident. It
is learned that he was drunk while driving and that he has been drinking a quart of alcohol per
day for the past 10 years. He is beginning to have delirium tremens. Blood studies and a diet
high in protein and calories are ordered for him.

25. Persons who have a long history of excessive drinking are *most likely* to manifest   25._____

    A. the development of a psychosis
    B. physical problems that require medical evaluation
    C. a need to deal with their problem on their own
    D. an inability to follow simple instructions

26. Which of these symptoms in Mr. Barnes would indicate that he is beginning to have an   26._____
episode of delirium tremens?

    A. Muscle rigidity, headache, and weeping
    B. Abdominal distention, stuttering, and lethargy
    C. Restlessness, tremulousness, and confusion
    D. Agitation, anger, and sarcasm

27. Mr. Barnes' behavior during delirium tremens is unsettling to his wife, who expresses   27.____
concern to the licensed practical nurse.
It would be BEST to convey to Mrs. Barnes that delirium tremens

   A.   happens when alcoholism is combined with a psychiatric disorder
   B.   is not serious and it usually disappears gradually within a few weeks
   C.   is not basically a serious disturbance, but the effects tend to be long-lasting
   D.   is frightening to observe, but it is usually temporary and subsides within a few days

28. As Mr. Barnes recovers from delirium tremens, he repeatedly makes demands of the   28.____
licensed practical nurse. Which of these actions should the nurse take?

   A.   Point out to Mr. Barnes that his behavior suggests that he could now benefit from
        attending meetings of Alcoholics Anonymous
   B.   Tell Mr. Barnes that he is demonstrating an abnormal degree of dependency
   C.   Recognize that Mr. Barnes may be troubled and take time to talk with him
   D.   Let Mr. Barnes know that his behavior is unreasonable and that the staff is trying to
        be tolerant

29. Hemoglobin and hematocrit determinations are ordered for Mr. Barnes to ascertain the   29.____
presence of

   A.   leukemia   B.   uremia   C.   erythema   D.   anemia

30. In view of the order for a diet high in protein and calories for Mr. Barnes, which of these   30.____
menus would be BEST for him?

   A.   Bacon, lettuce, and tomato sandwich, fruited gelatin dessert with whipped topping,
        and cola drink
   B.   Hot roast beef sandwich with gravy, mashed potatoes, green beans, chocolate
        pudding, and fruit punch
   C.   Beefburger patty, cucumber slald, cooked carrots, apple, and orange juice
   D.   Macaroni with tomato sauce, spinach, pear, and milk

KEY (CORRECT ANSWERS)

1.	B		16.	D
2.	A		17.	A
3.	A		18.	B
4.	A		19.	C
5.	C		20.	A
6.	D		21.	B
7.	A		22.	D
8.	B		23.	A
9.	D		24.	C
10.	A		25.	B
11.	C		26.	C
12.	B		27.	D
13.	A		28.	C
14.	C		29.	D
15.	D		30.	B

EXAMINATION SECTION
TEST 1

DIRECTIONS: Each question or incomplete statement is followed by several suggested answers or completions. Select the one that BEST answers the question or completes the statement. *PRINT THE LETTER OF THE CORRECT ANSWER IN THE SPACE AT THE RIGHT.*

1. A female patient who is terminally ill is working through her feelings about dying. The degree to which the licensed practical nurse can give support to this patient will be determined by the

    A. ability of the nurse to adhere to hospital policy regarding care of dying patients
    B. physician's willingness to prepare the patient for death
    C. age of the patient and the frequency with which the nurse has to give support to the dying
    D. nurse's feelings about death and the quality of the nurse's relationship with the patient

1.____

2. Which of these foods are good sources of vitamin A?

    A. Roast beef and bacon
    C. Orange juice and bananas
    B. Corn and yellow beans
    D. Carrots and sweet potatoes

2.____

3. The urine of a patient with high levels of bilirubin in the blood can be expected to be which of these colors?

    A. Clear yellow
    C. Red
    B. Dark amber
    D. Green

3.____

4. Which of these understandings should a licensed practical nurse have regarding the treatment and prognosis of glaucoma?

    A. Blindness will eventually develop, but treatment will delay it
    B. Vision already lost cannot be restored, and continuous treatment is necessary to prevent further visual loss
    C. Special eyeglasses will correct the visual impairment that occurs, but the lenses must be changed frequently
    D. Surgery can restore lost vision

4.____

5. Which of these measures is essential in the care of a patient who is in a coma?

    A. Checking the patient's blood pressure every 2 hours
    B. Maintaining the patient in a semi-Fowler's position
    C. Turning the patient from side to side at regular intervals
    D. Addressing the patient in a loud tone

5.____

6. During the first few hours after having a liver biopsy, the patient should be observed for which of these complications?

    A. Gastric irritation
    C. Allergic reactions
    B. Infection
    D. Hemorrhage

6.____

7. Colostomy irrigations have been ordered for a patient.   7._____
Which of these understandings is essential for safe performance of a colostomy irrigation?

    A. Absorption of the irrigating fluid in the intestinal tract will be affected by the patient's position
    B. The pressure of the irrigating fluid in the intestinal tract will be determined by the height at which the fluid container is held
    C. The irrigating fluid dilates the blood vessels of the intestinal tract
    D. Manipulation of the irrigation catheter results in muscle spasm of the intestinal tract

8. Emotional crises are *usually* MOST closely related to which of these aspects of a person's life?   8._____

    A. Interpersonal relationships
    B. Ethnic identification
    C. Religious beliefs
    D. Educational background

9. The licensed practical nurse should know that a Pap (Papanicolaou) test is a(n)   9._____

    A. biopsy of the vaginal wall to detect pathologic changes
    B. study of cervical cells to detect atypical cells
    C. uterine smear to detect endometritis
    D. examination to detect pelvic infection

QUESTIONS 10-16.

Miss Geraldine Froccaro, 43 years old, goes to her physician because she has not been feeling well. A tentative diagnosis of hyperthyroidism is made, and diagnostic tests are to be done in the ambulatory care center.

10. Which of these symptoms would Miss Froccaro *most likely* have as a result of an increase in the secretion of thyroxine?   10._____

    A. Loss of appetite and abnormal pigmentation
    B. Insomnia and palpitations
    C. Polyuria and excessive thirst
    D. Diaphoresis and disorientation

11. The results of which of these diagnostic tests may be used to confirm a diagnosis of hyperthyroidism?   11._____

    A. Protein-bound iodine and radioactive T-3 red cell uptake
    B. Flat plate of the chest and brain scan
    C. Thyroid scan and hemoglobin
    D. Electroencephalogram and electrocardiogram

12. As a result of an enlargement of Miss Froccaro's thyroid gland, which of these symptoms may occur?   12._____

    A. Feeling of pressure on the trachea
    B. Sensation of tickling in the oropharynx

    C. Impairment of hearing
    D. Pain over the sternum

A diagnosis of hyperthyroidism is confirmed.

13. Carbohydrates are very important in Miss Froccaro's diet at this time because they   13.____

    A. are easily stored by the body
    B. are easy to digest
    C. provide amino acids
    D. provide a readily available source of energy

14. In the treatment of patients with hyperthyroidism, which of these medications is likely to   14.____
    be prescribed to *decrease* the activity of the thyroid gland?

    A. Diazepam (Valium)
    B. Liothyronine sodium (Cytomel)
    C. Prednisone
    D. Propylthiouracil

Miss Froccaro is admitted to the hospital and she has a subtotal thyroidectomy. She is returned
to the surgical unit after a short stay in the recovery room. She is receiving fluids intravenously.

15. When Miss Froccaro has completely reacted from anesthesia and her vital signs are sta-   15.____
    ble, which of these positions would be BEST for her?

    A. Prone   B. Semi-Fowler's
    C. Trendelenburg   D. Supine

16. Which of the following information about Miss Froccaro's intravenous therapy will it be   16.____
    essential for the licensed practical nurse to have? The

    A. specific purpose of giving Miss Froccaro intravenous fluids
    B. total amount of intravenous fluid in the bottle
    C. desired rate of flow of the intravenous infusion
    D. amount of urine Miss Froccaro can be expected to excrete in relation to the amount
        of fluid that she is receiving intravenously

QUESTIONS 17-19.

Mr. Ed Adler, 35 years old, is admitted to the hospital. Mr. Adler has acute pyelonephritis.
Orders for Mr. Adler include bed rest, fluids ad lib., blood chemistry tests, and urine for culture
and sensitivity testing.

17. Mr. Adler is to be on bed rest in order to   17.____

    A. prevent respiratory infection by reducing his contact with other persons
    B. insure safety while his body has increased toxins in the bloodstream
    C. assist his body's defenses in combating infection
    D. control ascending urinary infection by maintaining him in a horizontal position

18. To obtain a urine specimen for culture from Mr. Adler, which of these actions is ESSEN-   18.____
    TIAL?

    A. Encourage him to drink fluids before his urine is collected
    B. Place a preservative in the receptacle in which his urine is to be collected
    C. Collect the first urine that he voids in the morning
    D. Use aseptic technique in collecting his urine

19. Mr. Adler's fluid intake and output are being measured. At breakfast Mr. Adler drank 6   19.____
    ounces of coffee and $4\frac{1}{2}$ ounces of orange juice.
    How many milliliters of fluid did he drink?

    A. 135   B. 205   C. 245   D. 315

QUESTIONS 20-32.

Mrs. Judith Bongo, 65 years old, complains of coldness, numbness, and tingling sensations in her lower extremities. There is an area of ulceration on her left ankle. After an examination by her physician, Mrs. Bongo is admitted to the hospital with peripheral vascular disease and diabetes mellitus. Her admission orders include bed rest and warm, moist packs to the ulcer site.

20. The licensed practical nurse who is admitting Mrs. Bongo should make certain that which   20.____
    of these items is added to her bed?

    A. Bed board   B. Bed cradle
    C. Shock blocks   D. Trapeze bar

21. In applying the moist packs to Mrs. Bongo's ankle, the licensed practical nurse should   21.____
    use aseptic technique in order to

    A. destroy bacteria on the skin
    B. inhibit the growth of pathogens
    C. prevent the introduction of additional microorganisms
    D. minimize the risk of spreading infection to others

22. The licensed practical nurse should observe MOST closely which of these properties of   22.____
    the moist packs that are used for Mrs. Bongo?

    A. Temperature   B. Size
    C. Type of solution   D. Type of dressing

23. Symptoms *most likely* to occur in people who have untreated diabetes mellitus include   23.____

    A. anorexia and constipation
    B. tremors and irritability
    C. excessive thirst and voiding of large amounts of urine
    D. excessive weight gain and excessive perspiration

The physician orders a 1,500-calorie diabetic diet for Mrs. Bongo and 30 units of isophane (NPH) insulin U-100 daily.

24. Mrs. Bongo is to have a midafternoon snack of milk and crackers.
The purpose of this measure for her is to

    A. improve nutrition
    B. improve carbohydrate metabolism
    C. prevent an insulin reaction
    D. prevent diabetic coma

24.____

25. Insulin is administered in the treatment of diabetes mellitus in order to

    A. stimulate the secretion of insulin in the body
    B. meet the metabolic need for insulin
    C. depress the activity of beta cells of the pancreas
    D. suppress the production of glycogen

25.____

26. Mrs. Bongo asks, "What's the difference between oral insulin and insulin by injection?"
The licensed practical nurse's reply should be based on the fact that

    A. oral drugs used for diabetes mellitus are not insulin
    B. oral drugs used for diabetes mellitus act more rapidly than insulin by injection
    C. an oral drug is a natural product whereas insulin for injection is a synthetic product
    D. there is no difference between the oral drug and insulin for injection

26.____

27. Mrs. Bongo is taught to test her urine for sugar four times a day.
At which of these times should the test be done?

    A. Upon arising in the morning and after meals
    B. Before meals and at bedtime
    C. Every six hours
    D. Between meals, at 8 P.M., and at midnight

27.____

28. Mrs. Bongo is being observed for symptoms of insulin reaction. Early symptoms of insulin reaction include

    A. abdominal pain and nausea
    B. dyspnea and pallor
    C. flushing of the skin and headache
    D. perspiration and a trembling sensation

28.____

29. The licensed practical nurse enters Mrs. Bongo's room as Mrs. Bongo is lighting a cigarette. She tells the nurse that her physician has advised her to stop smoking, and she asks, "Do you think it's all right if I cut down to smoking four or five cigarettes a day?"
The nurse's response should be based on which of these understandings about smoking cigarettes?

    A. Nicotine in cigarettes is a vasoconstrictor
    B. Cigarettes are carcinogenic
    C. Smoking is a bronchial irritant
    D. Smoking causes arteriosclerosis

29.____

30. To take care of her feet properly, Mrs. Bongo needs to know that it is necessary to   30._____

    A. soak her feet daily in water containing magnesium sulfate (Epsom salt)
    B. cut her toenails straight across
    C. remove calluses as soon as possible
    D. apply lotion liberally, especially between the toes

31. Before Mrs. Bongo's teaching program is completed, it will be important for her to have   31._____
which of these understandings about managing her diabetes mellitus?

    A. Sugar-free urine is the best indicator of the control of diabetes mellitus
    B. Diabetes mellitus can be cured if the measures prescribed by the physician are fol-
lowed closely
    C. Self-regulation of insulin dosage is the primary goal
    D. Symptoms of any illness warrant the immediate notification of the physician

32. Mrs. Bongo should be instructed to recognize the common early symptoms of diabetic   32._____
acidosis, which include

    A. thirst and drowsiness
    B. cold, clammy skin and anxiety
    C. slow pulse and increased blood pressure
    D. bulging of the eyeballs and dark amber urine

QUESTIONS 33-35.

Mr. Eugene Nussbaum, a 20-year-old college student, has difficulty in swallowing, an elevated
temperature, and chronic fatigue. He is admitted to the hospital. The results of diagnostic tests
reveal that Mr. Nussbaum has infectious mononucleosis with liver involvement. His orders
include a diet high in calories, protein, and vitamins.

33. Because of the liver involvement, Mr. Nussbaum should be expected to have which of   33._____
these symptoms?

    A. Constipation   B. Excessive thirst
    C. Anorexia   D. Hematuria

34. Mr. Nussbaum develops stomatitis. His mouth care should include which of these mea-   34._____
sures?

    A. Rinsing his mouth with an astringent mouthwash
    B. Cleansing his mouth frequently with a nonabrasive material
    C. Applying mineral oil to his irritated mucosa
    D. Coating his oral cavity with an antiseptic solution

35. Which of these behaviors is characteristic of a normal adolescent of Mr. Nussbaum's   35._____
age?

    A. Conforming to adult standards
    B. Worrying about athletic ability
    C. Having conflicts between dependence and independence
    D. Having definite vocational goals

KEY (CORRECT ANSWERS)

1.	D	16.	C
2.	D	17.	C
3.	B	18.	D
4.	B	19.	D
5.	C	20.	B
6.	D	21.	C
7.	B	22.	A
8.	A	23.	C
9.	B	24.	C
10.	B	25.	B
11.	A	26.	A
12.	A	27.	B
13.	D	28.	D
14.	D	29.	A
15.	B	30.	B

31.	B
32.	A
33.	C
34.	B
35.	C

EXAMINATION SECTION
TEST 1

DIRECTIONS: Each question or incomplete statement is followed by several suggested answers or completions. Select the one that BEST answers the question or completes the statement. *PRINT THE LETTER OF THE CORRECT ANSWER IN THE SPACE AT THE RIGHT.*

1. All of the following features usually favor the diagnosis of preeclampsia over essential hypertension EXCEPT   1.____

   A. family history negative
   B. onset of hypertension during the first 20 weeks of pregnancy
   C. primigravida
   D. proteinuria

2. The one of the following that is NOT considered a danger sign for pregnancy-induced hypertension is   2.____

   A. weight gain
   B. marked hyperreflexia, especially transient or sustained ankle clonus
   C. severe headache
   D. rapid rise of blood pressure and generalized edema

3. To teach a woman how to assess for pregnancy-induced hypertension, teach her to   3.____

   A. make a weight assessment every day and watch for an increase of 2 or more pounds per week
   B. observe for pitting edema of lower extremities, tight rings, shoes, and facial puffiness
   C. use a dipstick for assessment of proteinuria
   D. all of the above

4. The general health care plan of a woman with pregnancy-induced hypertension advises that she remain in bed.
In order to aid in enforcing this suggestion, a nurse should   4.____

   A. explain to her the importance of remaining in bed
   B. teach her relaxation techniques
   C. assess her family and internal support systems
   D. all of the above

5. Magnesium sulphate is given for the prevention of eclampsia in a pre-eclamptic woman. Danger signs for both the fetus and mother associated with magnesium sulphate toxicity include all of the following EXCEPT   5.____

   A. urinary output less than 25 ml/hr
   B. respiratory rate of more than 22/min.
   C. sudden hypotension
   D. sudden decrease in fetal heart rate

6. The antidote for toxicity of magnesium sulphate is

    A. sodium bicarbonate   B. calcium carbonate
    C. calcium gluconate   D. potassium chloride

6.____

7. The immediate care during a convulsion in an eclamptic woman is to ensure a patent air-way.
Nursing care of a woman with convulsions does NOT include

    A. keeping the woman supine to prevent aspiration of vomitus and hypotension
    B. inserting folded towel, plastic airway, or padded tongue blade into side of mouth to prevent biting of lips or tongue and to maintain airway
    C. suctioning food and fluid from glottis or trachea
    D. administering oxygen by means of face mask or tent after convulsion ceases

7.____

8. To monitor and minimize the severity of disease and effects of edema, proteinuria and hypertension in a woman with severe preeclampsia, the nurse should

    A. keep the woman on absolute bedrest with side rails up
    B. start IV and maintain rate to keep line open
    C. have the woman select people she wishes to stay with her and limit other visitors
    D. all of the above

8.____

9. To prevent adverse sequelae to severe PIH, the nurse should

    A. control the amount of external stimuli
    B. monitor symptoms and access level of consciousness and reflexes
    C. record findings of fundoscopic examination
    D. all of the above

9.____

10. To check urinary elimination in a patient with severe preeclampsia, the nurse should do all of the following EXCEPT

    A. keep accurate intake and output records
    B. check urine for glucose every 4 hours
    C. report output of less than 100 ml/4 hours
    D. send blood specimen to laboratory for measurement of creatinine

10.____

11. To monitor the severity of maternal response to PIH, the nurse should make assess-ments twice a week to note changes. She would NOT be assessing changes in

    A. glycosuria
    B. vital signs and blood pressure
    C. proteinuria
    D. edema and weight gain

11.____

12. To prevent further seizure in a woman with severe pre-eclampsia, the nurse should

    A. assess CNS status periodically and look for level of consciousness, fundoscopic changes, etc.
    B. assess for impending seizures and look for ankle clonus, epigastric pain, oliguria, etc.
    C. decrease environmental stimuli
    D. all of the above

12.____

13. All of the following are diseases spread by bodily contact but not necessarily by coitus   13.____
    EXCEPT

    A. pediculosis   B. molluscum contagiosum
    C. giardiasis   D. scabies

14. To treat an infected mother and newborn, the nurse should   14.____

    A. obtain specimen ordered for laboratory testing
    B. ensure adequate rest and nutrition
    C. provide high risk care to infant
    D. all of the above

15. Toxic shock syndrome is a potentially life-threatening systemic disorder MOST probably   15.____
    caused by

    A. toxin secreted by strains of S. aureus
    B. endotoxin secreted by E. coli
    C. enterococci
    D. salmonella toxin

16. Commonly associated conditions that may predispose a person to toxic shock syndrome   16.____
    by providing a portal of entry into systemic circulation include

    A. use of high-absorbency tampons or barrier contraceptives
    B. skin infection following a bee sting
    C. intravenous injection of heroin
    D. all of the above

17. Among the danger signs of toxic shock is   17.____

    A. fever of sudden onset, over 102° F
    B. hypotension, systolic pressure less than 90 mmHg
    C. rash, diffuse macular erythrodema
    D. all of the above

18. α-fetoprotein levels are measured at 16 weeks.   18.____
    All of the following conditions lead to elevated α-feto-protein level EXCEPT

    A. omphalocele   B. Down's syndrome
    C. multiple gestation   D. duodenal atresia

19. All of the following are routinely done in the third trimester of pregnancy EXCEPT   19.____

    A. repeat hemoglobin or hematocrit level
    B. α-fetoprotein measurement
    C. repeat antibody testing in unsensitized RH-negative patients at 28-32 weeks
    D. prophylactic RH_0 (anti-D) immune globulin administration, to reduce incidence of
        RH isoimmunization in an RH negative woman with a negative antibody screen
        and an RH positive husband

20. In an uncomplicated pregnancy, office visits of the pregnant woman do NOT need to be scheduled   20.____

    A. every four weeks for the first 28-30 weeks of pregnancy
    B. every 2 weeks from 30-36 weeks of pregnancy
    C. weekly from 36th week until delivery
    D. daily from 36th week until delivery

21. With real-time ultrasonography, fetal heart activity can be seen as early as _____ after the first missed menses.   21.____

    A. 2-3 weeks   B. 4-5 days
    C. 1 week   D. 5-6 weeks

22. During a routine office visit, a pregnant woman should be examined to gather information about the fetus, including   22.____

    A. fetal heart rate
    B. size of fetus and amount of amniotic fluid
    C. presenting part and station
    D. all of the above

23. It is unreasonable to advise rigid caloric restriction during pregnancy.
The recommended weight gain during pregnancy is_____ lbs.   23.____

    A. 5-10   B. 10-15   C. 20-30   D. 35-45

24. It was advocated in the past that sodium intake should be restricted in a pregnant woman.
This concept has been overruled because of the   24.____

    A. use of diuretics
    B. natriuretic effect of progesterone
    C. effect of prolactin
    D. reduction in dietary intake as general awareness develops in pregnant women

25. Folic acid is required in the formation of heme, the iron containing protein of hemoglobin. Folate deficiency in the pregnant woman may cause all of the following EXCEPT   25.____

    A. intrauterine growth retardation
    B. abruptio placentae
    C. pregnancy-induced hypertension
    D. anencephaly

KEY (CORRECT ANSWERS)

1.	B		11.	A
2.	A		12.	D
3.	D		13.	C
4.	D		14.	D
5.	B		15.	A
6.	C		16.	D
7.	A		17.	D
8.	D		18.	B
9.	D		19.	B
10.	B		20.	D

21.	A
22.	D
23.	C
24.	B
25.	A

TEST 2

DIRECTIONS: Each question or incomplete statement is followed by several suggested answers or completions. Select the one that BEST answers the question or completes the statement. *PRINT THE LETTER OF THE CORRECT ANSWER IN THE SPACE AT THE RIGHT.*

1. Nursing intervention to teach women about diabetes mellitus, its management, and its effects on pregnancy would NOT include   1._____

   A. reviewing the pathophysiology of the disease and clarifying any misconceptions
   B. teaching home monitoring tests, demonstrating techniques of interpretation, and recording of results
   C. reviewing effects of diabetes on pregnant woman and fetus and stressing weekly prenatal visits during the second half of pregnancy
   D. injection techniques

2. To assist a woman in verbalizing her concerns and adjusting to the strict management of diabetes, a nurse should NOT   2._____

   A. discuss the issues quickly in a hurried way
   B. provide consistency in caregivers and encourage verbalization of concerns and feelings
   C. compliment the woman on successful learning, problem solving, and coping
   D. refer her to a community diabetes support group

3. When teaching a diabetic woman about insulin, its effects on the body, and its proper administration, a nurse should do all of the following EXCEPT   3._____

   A. review the actions of insulin on the body and signs of hypoglycemia
   B. explain the importance of fixation to a particular site, which is always supposed to be used for insulin injection
   C. monitor the woman's self-administration of insulin until techniques are learned and understood
   D. teach proper techniques of insulin storage

4. To teach a diabetic woman about hyperglycemia, a nurse would NOT   4._____

   A. explain that any other illness, infection, vomiting, and diarrhea can precipitate keto-acidosis
   B. encourage the woman to call a physician when illness occurs and continue to administer insulin
   C. teach the danger signs of keto-acidosis
   D. instruct the patient to avoid fruit juice

5. To teach a diabetic woman on insulin therapy about hypo-glycemia, a nurse should NOT   5._____

   A. teach the signs and symptoms of hypoglycemia and review the causes and dangers of insulin reaction
   B. stress the importance of carrying fast-acting sugar when traveling and of having milk on hand at home
   C. review the relationship of exercise and diet
   D. tell the patient to read books to learn about it

6. Nursing intervention to teach a diabetic woman about diabetes diet management during pregnancy should do all of the following EXCEPT

    6.____

    A. consider cultural and financial implications when planning teaching
    B. stress the importance of losing weight during pregnancy
    C. explain the importance of a balanced diet and refer the woman to a registered dietician
    D. encourage the woman to design sample menus

7. To identify and treat infection in a pregnant woman with gestational diabetes, the one of the following that the nurse would NOT do is

    7.____

    A. teach the woman to understand the signs and symptoms of infection, either locally or systemically
    B. obtain specimens for culture
    C. explain that infection decreases insulin resistance and keto-acidosis
    D. administer prophylactic antibiotic as ordered

8. Certain factors may place a woman and fetus at risk for problems during pregnancy. When obtaining preconception health history, the nurse should be expecially alert for all of the following demographic factors so she can help prevent potential problems EXCEPT

    8.____

    A. age 15 or below and 35 or above
    B. high socio-economic status
    C. location in rural or isolated area and lack of transportation
    D. non-white and unmarried

9. Which of the following factors in the obstetric history places the woman and fetus at risk for problems during pregnancy?

    9.____

    A. Previous spontaneous or elective abortion
    B. Previous premature neonate or neonate with a congenital anomaly
    C. Maternal anatomic difficulty, such as severe retro-flexed uterus or pelvis too small for normal delivery
    D. All of the above

10. Oral contraceptives inhibit ovulation by blocking the actions of the hypothalamus and anterior pituitary on the uterus.
Although oral contraceptives do have some disadvantages, they do NOT increase the risk of

    10.____

    A. endometrial and ovarian cancer, ovarian cysts, and noncancerous breast tumors
    B. thromboembolic disorders, cerebrovascular accidents, and sub-arachnoid hemorrhage, especially if the woman is a smoker or has hypertension
    C. monilia vaginitis
    D. hepatic lesions, including hepatic adenomas

11. All of the following are advantages of vaginal spermicide EXCEPT   11.____

    A. easy to insert
    B. must be inserted before each act of intercourse
    C. decreases risk of PID
    D. requires no prescription

12. All the steps of the nursing process should be documented. When caring for a couple   12.____
who request help with preconception planning, documentation should include

    A. significant health history and physical assessment findings
    B. results of diagnostic studies performed
    C. instructions given to the couple
    D. all of the above

13. History can reveal the risk of genetic disorders and may aid in diagnosing genetic disor-   13.____
ders.
Risk factors include all of the following EXCEPT

    A. previous birth of an affected child
    B. woman under 35 years of age and history of one abortion or stillbirth
    C. family history of genetic defects
    D. intrauterine exposure to known teratogens

14. The woman at increased risk for bearing a child with a genetic defect may need assis-   14.____
tance in deciding on reproductive alternatives.
Before becoming pregnant, she may need to choose among different options, but it is
NOT necessary for her to

    A. accept the risk and attempt pregnancy or avoid the risk and refrain from pregnancy
    B. minimize the risk by considering such alternatives as artificial insemination
    C. refrain from sex
    D. monitor the risk by undergoing prenatal diagnostic tests to identify an affected fetus

15. Genetic disorders or associated birth defects may place severe physical, psychological,   15.____
and economic strains on a woman and her family.
The nursing role in assisting a woman and her family in care management, referrals,
and successful adjustments include

    A. identifying physical or developmental abnormalities
    B. assessing the need for referrals to specialty services for genetic evaluations,
       genetic counseling, or prenatal diagnostic studies
    C. demonstrating sensitivity to the attitudes of a woman with a genetic disorder, espe-
       cially regarding reproduction
    D. all of the above

16. The fetal period involves growth and further development of organ systems established   16.____
in the embryonic period. The fetal period extends from week _____ to week _____.

    A. 8; 40   B. 12; 20   C. 18; 36   D. 12; 30

17. Fetal circulation differs from neonatal circulation in that three shunts bypass the liver and lungs and separate the systemic and pulmonary circulations.
NOT included among these shunts is the

    A. foramen of Monro   B. ductus venosus
    C. foramen ovale   D. ductus arteriosus

17.____

18. All of the following are possible causes of nausea and. vomiting in a suspected pregnant woman EXCEPT

    A. anorexia nervosa
    B. gastric disorders
    C. rising levels of HCG
    D. pseudocyesis

18.____

19. In a pregnant woman, the vaginal pH turns acidic, which helps prevent bacterial infection. This change in pH arises with increased production of lactic acid from glycogen in the vaginal epithelium.
Increased lactic acid results from the action of

    A. E. coli   B. lactobacillus acidophilus
    C. nessaria gonorrhea   D. trichomonas vaginalis

19.____

20. All of the following are functional changes in the urinary system as a result of pregnancy EXCEPT

    A. renal plasma flow rises to 40-50% above prepregnant level by the third trimester
    B. GFR starts declining by the beginning of the second trimester and remains low until term
    C. renal tubular resorption increases as much as 50% during pregnancy
    D. loss of increased amount of some nutrients, such as amino acids, water soluble vitamins, folic acid, and iodine

20.____

21. Which of the following is NOT a sign of fetal distress in a pregnant woman with insulin-dependent diabetes mellitus?

    A. A non-reactive NST
    B. Decreased insulin requirement
    C. Negative CST
    D. Poor biophysical profile

21.____

22. In a multiparous woman, pre-eclampsia may be associated with

    A. multiple gestation
    B. chronic hypertension
    C. diabetes and coexisting renal disease
    D. all of the above

22.____

23. Severe pregnancy-induced hypertension is manifested by all of the following EXCEPT

    A. diastolic blood pressure of 110 mmHg or more
    B. elevated creatinine
    C. 1+ proteinuria
    D. presence of thrombocytopenia and fetal growth retardation

23.____

24. Indications for delivery in a pregnant woman with pregnancy-induced hypertension include

24.____

    A. a compromise in fetal well-being, as manifested by poor biophysical profile, etc.
    B. worsening hypertension
    C. increasing proteinuria
    D. all of the above

25. Sickle cell anemia occurs when an individual receives the gene for the production of hemoglobin 5 from each parent.
Pregnancy is a serious burden in women with SS disease because of the likelihood of all of the following EXCEPT

25.____

    A. anemia becoming more intense
    B. infection and pulmonary dysfunction
    C. pain crises becoming more infrequent
    D. death of the woman and chils

KEY (CORRECT ANSWERS)

1.	D		11.	B
2.	A		12.	D
3.	B		13.	B
4.	D		14.	C
5.	D		15.	D
6.	B		16.	A
7.	C		17.	A
8.	B		18.	C
9.	D		19.	B
10.	A		20.	B

21.	C
22.	D
23.	C
24.	D
25.	C

TEST 3

DIRECTIONS: Each question or incomplete statement is followed by several suggested answers or completions. Select the one that BEST answers the question or completes the statement. *PRINT THE LETTER OF THE CORRECT ANSWER IN THE SPACE AT THE RIGHT.*

1. A 28-year-old primipara with a hemoglobin of 9.2 before becoming pregnant has a hemoglobin of 8 during her pregnancy, despite oral iron and folic acid supplementation. Her infant is born with a normal hemoglobin. This woman was suffering from

    A. hemoglobin SC disease   B. megaloblastic anemia
    C. iron deficiency anemia   D. sickle cell anemia

1.____

2. All of the following factors increase a pregnant woman's risk of contracting HIV infection and acquired immunodeficiency syndrome EXCEPT

    A. using illicit IV drugs or having a sexual partner who uses such drugs
    B. having frequent sex with the same partner
    C. receiving, or having a sexual partner who received, blood or blood products
    D. having a bisexual male partner

2.____

3. The one of the following changes that does NOT appear in a pregnant woman around the 23rd to 27th week is

    A. umbilicus appears level with abdominal skin
    B. Braxton Hicks contractions stop
    C. shape of uterus changes from globular to ovoid
    D. striae gravidarum usually become apparent

3.____

4. Most pregnant women can travel without undue risk to the fetus. However, risk of accident increases with the amount of traveling.
Recommended precautions include

    A. in moving vehicle, wear shoulder lap belts to reduce injury in case of accident
    B. do not remain seated for longer than 2 hours
    C. as term approaches, determine the availability of medical care at destination
    D. all of the above

4.____

5. Whether childbirth education occurs in client-teaching sessions with individuals or in classrooms with groups of clients and their parents, it should include education about the

    A. physiologic aspects of pregnancy and childbirth
    B. proper relaxation and breathing techniques
    C. transition to parenthood
    D. all of the above

5.____

6. For the normal antepartal initial visit, it is NOT necessary to document

    A. patient's vital signs, height, weight, age, occupation, and social history, including smoking, drugs, and alcohol
    B. the number of previous pregnancies and complications

6.____

C. how often sex is performed
D. any danger sign encountered, fetal activity, allergies to medication, and date of next visit

7. There are various risk factors during pregnancy that can affect nutrition. These factors include

7.____

A. pregnancy-induced hypertension
B. multiple gestation
C. inadequate or excessive weight gain
D. all of the above

8. A few nutritionally related blood tests typically are performed during pregnancy. These include all of the following EXCEPT

8.____

A. serum ceruloplasmin level
B. hemoglobin levels, hematocrit, mean corpuscular volume, and mean corpuscular hemoglobin concentration
C. a fasting 1 hour glucose tolerance test at 24-28 weeks gestation to screen for gestational diabetes
D. serum albumin levels

9. Basic goals for nutrition throughout pregnancy include

9.____

A. adjusting dietary intake to promote appropriate weight gain
B. increasing nutrient intake to meet the RDA's for pregnancy
C. establishing an appropriate food intake pattern for nutritionally-related problems such as anemia and nausea
D. all of the above

10. In the general teaching plan of a pregnant woman, which of the following dietary plans will NOT be recommended to maximize iron uptake from food?

10.____

A. Drink tea or coffee as they increase iron absorption
B. Eat poultry, fish, and meat often to provide easily absorbable iron
C. Cook with iron pots and pans
D. Eat iron-rich vegetables, such as spinach, broccoli, asparagus, and other dark green vegetables

11. The hyperglycemia and insulin deficiency associated with diabetes mellitus produce all of the following classical signs and symptoms of diabetes EXCEPT

11.____

A. polyuria
B. polydipsia and polyphagia
C. dysphagia
D. weight loss

12. Iron deficiency anemia in a pregnant woman will NOT produce

12.____

A. spontaneous abortion and stillbirth
B. decreased fetal iron stores
C. fetal distress from hypoxia during later pregnancy and labor
D. neonate small for gestational age

13. Sickle cell anemia is diagnosed in a pregnant woman.   13.____
    She can expect all of the following complications EXCEPT

    A. pulmonary emboli
    B. excessive bleeding after delivery
    C. urinary tract infection
    D. pregnancy-induced hypertension

14. Sickle cell anemia in a pregnant woman will NOT lead to   14.____

    A. abruptio placentae complications
    B. prematurity
    C. large for gestational age neonate
    D. intrauterine growth retardation

15. As a result of folic acid deficiency, _____ can be expected in a pregnant woman.   15.____

    A. urinary tract infection
    B. bleeding complications during delivery
    C. pancytopenia
    D. all of the above

16. _____ is NOT expected in a pregnant woman as a result of iron deficiency anemia.   16.____

    A. Poor tissue integrity
    B. Pulmonary emboli
    C. Excessive bleeding after delivery
    D. Antepartal or postpartal infection with impaired healing

17. All of the following fetal and neonate complications are expected as a result of maternal   17.____
    toxoplasmosis EXCEPT

    A. premature and/or stillbirth
    B. hypertonia
    C. blindness, deafness, or chorioretinitis
    D. mental retardation, seizures, and coma

18. Nursing intervention in the prevention of maternal toxoplasmosis includes advising the   18.____
    woman to

    A. cook meat thoroughly to kill bacteria
    B. avoid contact with cat box filler, especially if the cats roam outside
    C. wear gloves while gardening
    D. all of the above

19. All of the following fetal and neonatal complications are expected in a pregnant woman   19.____
    with cytomegalovirus infection EXCEPT

    A. macrocephaly
    B. neonatal jaundice and hepatosplenomegaly
    C. hearing loss and blindness
    D. mental retardation, cerebral palsy, and epilepsy

20. A nurse treating a pregnant woman with cytomegalovirus infection should   20.____

    A. be aware that CMV can be transmitted by any close contact, including kissing and sexual intercourse

    B. advise the infected woman not to breastfeed her neonate because the virus can be transmitted through breast milk

    C. expect to isolate the mother and neonate after birth

    D. all of the above

21. Spontaneous abortion may occur as a result of rubella infection in a pregnant woman.   21.____
The fetal and neonatal complications expected as a result of rubella infection include

    A. cardiac defects, such as pulmonary artery stenosis and patent ductus arteriosus

    B. intrauterine growth retardation

    C. deafness, cataracts, glaucoma, and mental retardation

    D. all of the above

22. For the prevention of rubella infection, it is CORRECT that   22.____

    A. it is alright for a pregnant woman to have contact with people known to have rubella

    B. a negative antibody titer indicates that the woman is immune to rubella

    C. it is alright for the woman to become pregnant within 1 year after receiving the vaccine

    D. it is not necessary for her to obtain rubella vaccination after delivery

23. Nursing intervention while dealing with a woman having vaginal candidiasis includes   23.____

    A. telling the patient to practice thorough perineal hygiene

    B. teaching the patient about candidiasis and supporting her during occurrences

    C. assessing the neonate after delivery for signs of thrush, such as creamy, white, slightly elevated plaque inside the mouth

    D. all of the above

24. All of the following are fetal and neonatal complications of ethanol consumption in a   24.____
pregnant woman EXCEPT

    A. intrauterine growth retardation

    B. long palpebral fissures and macrocephaly

    C. irritability and poor coordination

    D. mild to moderate mental retardation

25. Complications expected in a pregnant woman as a result of cocaine abuse include   25.____

    A. dilated pupils and muscle twitching

    B. cardiac and respiratory arrest

    C. increased spontaneous abortion, abruptio placentae, and pre-term labor

    D. all of the above

KEY (CORRECT ANSWERS)

1.	C		11.	C
2.	B		12.	B
3.	B		13.	B
4.	D		14.	C
5.	D		15.	D
6.	C		16.	B
7.	D		17.	B
8.	A		18.	D
9.	D		19.	A
10.	A		20.	D

21.	D
22.	C
23.	D
24.	B
25.	D

————

EXAMINATION SECTION
TEST 1

DIRECTIONS: Each question or incomplete statement is followed by several suggested answers or completions. Select the one that BEST answers the question or completes the statement. *PRINT THE LETTER OF THE CORRECT ANSWER IN THE SPACE AT THE RIGHT.*

1. Symptoms characteristic of severe preeclampsia include   1.____

   A. ringing in the ears and rapid pulse
   B. elevated temperature and excitability
   C. vomiting and excessive urination
   D. persistent headache and blurred vision

2. In the care of a newborn with hydrocephalus, which of these measures is *especially* important?   2.____

   A. Keeping the baby dry
   B. Changing the baby's position at regular intervals
   C. Feeding the baby small amounts of formula frequently
   D. Placing the baby so that his head is lower than the rest of his body

3. A newborn who has a cleft palate is to be bottle-fed.   3.____
   Which of these measures would it be MOST important to take when feeding this infant?

   A. Apply elbow restraints to the infant prior to each feeding
   B. Hold the infant in an upright position during feedings
   C. Give the infant a small amount of sterile water after each feeding
   D. Feed the infant small amounts frequently

QUESTIONS 4-12.

Mrs. Connie Tong, 21 years old, attends the antepartal clinic. The physician examines Mrs. Tong and finds her to be about 3 months pregnant.

4. The licensed practical nurse is talking with Mrs. Tong about her nutritional needs.   4.____
   The nurse should advise Mrs. Tong that she will get the HIGHEST amount of vitamins and minerals from the vegetables in her diet if she

   A. eats them raw
   B. stores them in the refrigerator
   C. cooks them in unsalted water
   D. boils them in a covered pot

5. Mrs. Tong says to the licensed practical nurse, "I try to drink as much milk as I'm sup-   5.____
   posed to, but it's hard to do because I don't like milk."
   Which of these responses by the nurse would be BEST?

   A. Ask Mrs. Tong what foods she likes that contain milk
   B. Ask Mrs. Tong if she understands why milk is important for the development of her baby

    C.   Suggest that Mrs. Tong substitute one whole egg for every glass of milk that she omits from her diet

    D.   Suggest that Mrs. Tong talk with her physician about taking calcium tablets as a substitute for milk

6.   During Mrs. Tong's clinic visit when she is 4 months pregnant, which of these procedures will be carried out for her?   6.____

    A.   Vaginal smear and pelvic measurements
    B.   Vaginal examination and Rh factor determination
    C.   Blood test for syphilis and rectal examination
    D.   Blood pressure determination and weighing

7.   Which of these understandings regarding activity for pregnant women would it be BEST for the licensed practical nurse to have?   7.____

    A.   Activities that require stretching and bending should be avoided
    B.   Usual activities should be continued in moderation
    C.   Emphasis should be given to active participation in outdoor activities
    D.   Each new activity should be preceded by a short period of rest

Mrs. Tong's pregnancy progresses normally. She is admitted to the hospital at term in early active labor.

8.   Which of these occurences is the MOST reliable indication of the onset of true labor?   8.____

    A.   The woman's report of a burst of energy
    B.   Regular progression of uterine contractions
    C.   Increased vaginal discharge
    D.   Rupture of the membranes

Mrs. Tong has a normal spontaneous delivery of a girl. Mrs. Tong plans to breast-feed her infant.

9.   When Mrs. Tong is 6 hours postpartum, she is placed on a bedpan to void. After trying for a period of time, Mrs. Tong states that she is unable to void. Her bladder is distended. Which of these measures would it be BEST for the licensed practical nurse to use to help Mrs. Tong to void?   9.____

    A.   Pour warm water over her vulva
    B.   Apply gentle manual pressure over her bladder
    C.   Encourage her to drink fluids freely
    D.   Explain to her that she will have to be catheterized if she does not void

10.   When Baby Girl Tong is brought to Mrs. Tong for the first breast-feeding, Mrs. Tong asks the licensed practical nurse, "How much of the nipple should the baby be given?" Which of these replies is it CORRECT for the nurse to give Mrs. Tong?   10.____

    A.   "The baby should have the nipple and some of the dark area around the nipple well into her mouth."

    B.   "Since she's had some water from a bottle in the nursery, she has already learned the amount of nipple she needs to nurse adequately."

    C.   "Babies' mouths are of different sizes, and the baby will take the correct amount of nipple for her."

    D.   "Babies nurse best when only the nipple is in the mouth."

11.   On Mrs. Tong's third postpartum day, the licensed practical nurse finds her crying. When asked what seems to be wrong, Mrs. Tong says, "I really don't know. I have so much to be grateful for – a healthy baby, a good husband – I really should be happy."
Which of these actions by the nurse would demonstrate the BEST judgment in this situation?   11._____

    A.   Provide privacy for Mrs. Tong

    B.   Ask Mrs. Tong if her relationship with her husband will permit her to discuss her feelings with him.

    C.   Explain to Mrs. Tong that her reaction is an unusual one

    D.   Remain with Mrs. Tong for a while

12.   Because Mrs. Tong is breast-feeding her baby, the diet recommended for her is likely to differ from that recommended for a mother who is NOT nursing by it being   12._____

    A.   lower in roughage, and higher in carbohydrates

    B.   lower in sodium, and higher in iron

    C.   higher in calcium and protein

    D.   higher in fat and cellulose

QUESTIONS 13-19.

Mrs. Merrilee Stone, 31 years old, comes to the antepartal clinic because she has missed 2 menstrual periods. She is found to be about 10 weeks pregnant. This is Mrs. Stone's third pregnancy. The Stones have 2 children.

13.   Mrs. Stone has been advised by the physician to increase her intake of iron.
Which of these sandwiches, as *ordinarily* prepared, is HIGHEST in iron?   13._____

    A.   Egg salad   B.   Peanut butter

    C.   Cream cheese and jelly   D.   Lettuce and tomato

Mrs. Stone attends the clinic when she is 8 months pregnant.

14.   Three of the following symptoms are common at this stage of pregnancy.
Which one is NOT?   14._____

    A.   Frequent urination   B.   Nausea and vomiting

    C.   Edema of the ankles   D.   Dyspnea when lying flat in bed

15.   Mrs. Stone says to the licensed practical nurse, "Sometimes I think about what would happen if I died during childbirth." Which of these approaches by the nurse would be BEST?   15._____

    A.   Explain to her that such thoughts are common at her stage of pregnancy

    B.   Tell her that maternal deaths are extremely rare

    C.   Find out what prompted these feelings in her

    D.   Ask her if she has discussed these feelings with her husband

At term Mrs. Stone is admitted to the hospital in active labor. Mrs. Stone's labor is being electronically monitored.

16. Which of these findings, if observed in Mrs. Stone, should be reported to the nurse in charge IMMEDIATELY?

    16.____

    A. A decrease in the fetal heart rate from 144 to 132 during a contraction
    B. A decrease in the interval between contractions from 6 to 7 minutes to 4 to 5 minutes
    C. A sudden increase in the amount of blood in the vaginal show
    D. An increase in blood pressure from 120/76 to 132/80 at the beginning of a contraction

17. The duration of Mrs. Stone's contractions should be timed from the

    17.____

    A. beginning of a contraction to the beginning of the next contraction
    B. beginning of a contraction to the end of that contraction
    C. end of a contraction to the beginning of the next contraction
    D. end of a contraction to the end of the next contraction

Mrs. Stone's labor progresses normally. She delivers a boy.

18. A few hours after Mrs. Stone's delivery, the licensed practical nurse notes that Mrs. Stone has saturated two perineal pads with blood within a 20-minute period. Which of these actions should the nurse take FIRST?

    18.____

    A. Check the consistency of Mrs. Stone's uterine fundus
    B. Encourage Mrs. Stone to void
    C. Take Mrs. Stone's blood pressure
    D. Notify the nurse in charge

Mrs. Stone is transferred to the postpartum unit.

19. Mrs. Stone says to the licensed practical nurse, "I guess I really want some help. I don't need any more children. Three are enough."
Which of these approaches by the nurse would be *best* FIRST?

    19.____

    A. Find out what Mrs. Stone knows about the availability of family planning services
    B. Ask Mrs. Stone if her husband is interested in conception control
    C. Discuss with Mrs. Stone the effectiveness of various contraceptive methods
    D. Commend Mrs. Stone for her determination to limit her family size

QUESTIONS 20-26.

Mrs. Ulule Braxton, 32 years old, has 6 children, aged 1, 2, 3, 5, 7, and 9 years. Mrs. Braxton is visiting the physician because she has not menstruated for several months.

20. In the waiting room, Mrs. Braxton says to another patient, "Here I am again. I kind of hope that I'm not pregnant." When the licensed practical nurse is helping Mrs. Braxton to prepare for her examination, the nurse says to Mrs. Braxton, "I overheard your comments to the other patient in the waiting room."
Which of these additional remarks by the nurse would be MOST appropriate to follow this initial comment?

    20.____

A. "You may feel negative about another pregnancy now. These feelings are bound to change."
B. "It's healthy to express your feelings. Let's talk about them."
C. "You ought to discuss these feelings with the doctor, since they may affect the outcome of your pregnancy."
D. "The doctor may advise you to seek professional counseling. Such feelings often precede emotional problems in the postpartum period."

Mrs. Braxton is about 3 months pregnant.

21. A presumptive diagnosis of pregnancy can be made at 3 months' gestation by   21.____

   A. hearing fetal heart tones via a fetoscope
   B. the presence of chorionic gonadotropin in the mother's urine
   C. seeing the fetal skeleton on an x-ray
   D. the mother's confirmation of quickening

22. Why is it especially IMPORTANT for Mrs. Braxton to be under medical supervision during   22.____
   her pregnancy?

   A. Premature labor is a common occurence in women such as Mrs. Braxton who are extremely active and over 25 years of age
   B. Fetal anoxia results from placental aging, which is common in women of Mrs. Braxton's age group
   C. Multigravidas are especially susceptible to infectious diseases
   D. Grand multiparas have a higher incidence of complications

At term Mrs. Braxton is admitted to the hospital and delivers a 9-lb., 4-oz. (4,196-gm.) boy. Mrs. Braxton is planning to breast-feed her baby.

23. At 5 minutes of life, Baby Boy Braxton's Apgar score is 9. Which of these findings is NOT   23.____
   present in babies with such a score?

   A. Pulse rate of 120
   B. Regular abdominal breathing
   C. Flaccidity of the lower extremities
   D. Crying in response to being physically stimulated

24. Three of the following drugs may be administered to Mrs. Braxton while she is in the   24.____
   delivery room.
   Which one would NOT be given to her since she is planning to breast-feed her infant?

   A. Oxytocin injection (Pitocin)
   B. Ergonovine maleate (Ergotrate)
   C. Methylergonovine (Methergine) maleate
   D. Testosterone enanthate and estradiol valerate (Deladumone)

25. Mrs. Braxton expresses concern about her ability to supply the baby with enough milk   25.____
   because of his large size.
   Which of these ideas should most certainly be included in the licensed practical nurse's response?

A. Supplemental feedings can be added for babies who weigh more than 9 pounds
B. Eight to ten glasses of fluid per day, half of which should be milk, will insure an adequate milk supply
C. Smoking should be avoided since it interferes with blood circulation in the mammary glands, thus reducing milk production
D. The more the baby sucks, the more milk the breasts will produce to meet the baby's needs

26. Mrs. Braxton asks the licensed practical nurse how effective oral contraceptive drugs are in preventing pregnancy. Which of these replies would be accurate? 26.____

A. "They are quite effective in women whose menstrual cycle is regular."
B. "They vary in effectiveness according to the woman's age."
C. "They are very effective when taken exactly as prescribed."
D. "They are highly effective only if used in conjunction with a birth control device such as a diaphragm."

QUESTIONS 27-36.

Mrs. Dolores Garcia is a 24-year-old multigravida who is 8 months pregnant. She comes to the hospital and is admitted to the labor room with bright red vaginal bleeding. The physician suspects that Mrs. Garcia may have placenta previa or abruptio placentae.

27. During the admission process, three of the following measures would be appropriate for Mrs. Garcia. Which one would be *contraindicated* for her? 27.____

A. Giving an enema
B. Obtaining a urine specimen
C. Checking for uterine contractions
D. Shaving the perineal area

28. When Mrs. Garcia is admitted, which of the following information should be obtained FIRST? 28.____

A. Her temperature and respiratory rate
B. Her blood pressure and pulse rate
C. Her height and weight
D. The date of her last menstrual period and the dates of her previous pregnancies

29. Which of these symptoms is *frequently* found in women with abruptic placentae, but is rare in women with placenta previa? 29.____

A. Thirst
B. Projectile vomiting
C. Abdominal pain
D. Small cysts in the vaginal discharge

It is determined that Mrs. Garcia has placenta previa, and a cesarean section is performed under spinal anesthesia. A 4-lb. (1,814-gm.) girl is delivered and is transferred to the premature nursery, where she is placed in an incubator. Mrs. Garcia is transferred from the recovery room to the postpartum unit with an intravenous infusion in her left arm and an indwelling urinary catheter attached to gravity drainage.

30. Identification tags were placed on both Baby Girl Garcia and her mother before they left   30.____
    the delivery room.
    The CHIEF reason this was done at that time is that

    A. it is the recommended hospital policy
    B. it is the most convenient time
    C. the procedure can be done under aseptic conditions
    D. the baby and her mother had not yet been separated

31. Mrs. Garcia is to be kept flat in bed for about 8 hours postoperatively.   31.____
    The purpose of this measure is to prevent

    A. headache   B. hemorrhage
    C. hypertension   D. pulmonary embolus

32. An hour after Mrs. Garcia is transferred to the postpartum unit, the licensed practical   32.____
    nurse notes that her blood pressure reading has changed from 120/80 to 96/70 and that
    her abdominal dressings are dry.
    Which of these actions should the nurse take FIRST?

    A. Massage Mrs. Garcia's uterine fundus
    B. Elevate the foot of Mrs. Garcia bed
    C. Check Mrs. Garcia's perineal pad
    D. Change Mrs. Garcia's position

33. Mrs. Garcia's indwelling urinary catheter is removed at 10 a.m. on the day after delivery.   33.____
    The time and amount of each of Mrs. Garcia's first three voidings after the catheter is
    removed are as follows: 5 p.m., 350 ml.; 11 p.m., 280 ml.; and 6 a.m., 370 ml.
    The licensed practical nurse should know about Mrs. Garcia's urinary pattern the
    amounts voided

    A. and the intervals between voidings are within normal limits
    B. are normal, but the intervals between voidings are above normal
    C. are above normal, nut the intervals between voidings are normal
    D. and the intervals between voidings are below normal

34. It is important for the mother of a premature infant to to have *early* contact with her   34.____
    baby because this practice

    A. reduces the mother's dependency needs
    B. stimulates the physical growth rate of the baby
    C. enhances the mother-infant relationship
    D. decreases the likelihood that postpartum blues might occur

35. Which of these statements is correct about breast engorgement and afterpains in Mrs.   35.____
    Garcia in comparison with multiparas who have delivered vaginally?

    A. She is likely to have breast engorgement and afterpains similar to those of women
       who delivered vaginally
    B. She is likely to have afterpains similar to those of women who delivered vaginally,
       but breast engorgement will be absent

C. Her breast engorgement will be similar to that of women who delivered vaginally, but afterpains will be absent
D. Her breast engorgement and her afterpains will be different from those of women who delivered vaginally

36. On Mrs. Garcia's sixth postpartum day, her lochia is bright red and moderate in amount. Which of these actions should the licensed practical nurse take FIRST?

    36.____

A. Encourage Mrs. Garcia to increase her ambulation in order to aid involution
B. Have Mrs. Garcia lie on her abdomen for about an hour in order to apply pressure to the uterus
C. Chart the observation
D. Report the observation to the nurse in charge

QUESTIONS 37-40.

Mrs. Abby Cunningham, 27 years old, is at a ski lodge when she goes into active labor. A severe blizzard has blocked all roads. No physician is available and the nearest hospital is 60 miles away. A licensed practical nurse who is also a guest at the lodge is called to assist Mrs. Cunningham. This is Mrs. Cunningham's second pregnancy.

37. The licensed practical nurse determines that the birth of the baby is imminent. Which of these actions should the nurse take during the delivery of the baby?

    37.____

A. Apply gentle pressure to Mrs. Cunningham's abdomen and tell her to push with each contraction
B. Support Mrs. Cunningham's perineum and the baby's head as it emerges
C. Tell Mrs. Cunningham to take slow, deep breaths during each contraction and to push between contractions
D. Place a clean towel under Mrs. Cunningham's buttocks and help her to hold her legs in lithotomy position

Mrs. Cunningham delivers a boy.

38. To promote a patent airway in the baby immediately after delivery, the licensed practical nurse should

    38.____

A. place him in a semisitting position
B. stimulate his swallowing reflex
C. hold his tongue forward
D. position his head lower than his body

39. After the delivery of the placenta, it will be ESSENTIAL for the licensed practical nurse to

    39.____

A. determine if involution has occured
B. see if pulsations of the umbilical cord have ceased
C. check the firmness of the uterine fundus
D. palpate the bladder area

40. If Mrs. Cunningham were to bleed heavily from perineal laceration, which of these actions would be appropriate?   40.____

    A. Place her in Trendelenburg position
    B. Apply pressure to the tear
    C. Massage the uterus
    D. Put the baby to breast

———

KEY (CORRECT ANSWERS)

1. D	11. D	21. B	31. A
2. B	12. C	22. D	32. C
3. B	13. A	23. C	33. A
4. A	14. B	24. D	34. C
5. A	15. C	25. D	35. A
6. D	16. C	26. C	36. D
7. B	17. B	27. A	37. B
8. B	18. A	28. B	38. D
9. A	19. A	29. C	39. C
10. A	20. B	30. D	40. B

———

EXAMINATION SECTION
TEST 1

DIRECTIONS: Each question or incomplete statement is followed by several suggested
answers or completions. Select the one that BEST answers the question or
completes the statement. *PRINT THE LETTER OF THE CORRECT ANSWER
IN THE SPACE AT THE RIGHT.*

1.   The prolactin hormone stimulated by breastfeeding in the postpartal period seems to
have an inhibitory effect on menstruation, by performing all of the following EXCEPT

    A.   supresses luteinizing hormone
    B.   supresses follicle-stimulating hormone
    C.   supresses estrogen
    D.   direct inhibitory effect on ovaries

1.____

2.   In the first 2-3 days postpartum, a 15-30 percent increase in circulating blood volume
results from
    I.   elimination of the placental circulation
    II.   decrease in venous return
    III.   shift of extracellular fluid into systemic circulation
The CORRECT answer is:

    A.   I and II   B.   I and III
    C.   II and III   D.   I, II, and III

2.____

3.   The mechanisms that prevent hemorrhage and are called upon at delivery to meet the
challenges of placental separation, episiotomy, and lacerations include

    A.   muscle contraction
    B.   tissue pressure
    C.   platelet and coagulation system activity
    D.   all of the above

3.____

4.   Women who have been found,during pregnancy,to have no immunity against rubella
should receive the vaccine in the postpartal period, usually on the day of discharge. Side
effects of the rubella vaccine include all of the following EXCEPT

    A.   mild athralgia   B.   rash
    C.   pericardial effusion   D.   elevated temperature

4.____

5.   Following an episode of hypovolemic shock caused by postpartum hemorrhage, necrosis
of an endocrine structure produced Sheehan's syndrome.
The endocrine structure involved is the

    A.   hypothalamus   B.   anterior pituitary
    C.   posterior pituitary   D.   adrenal medulla

5.____

6.   Since pituitary function influences other endocrine structures, Sheehan's syndrome may
produce all of the following signs and symptoms EXCEPT

6.____

A. lack of lactation
B. signs of thyroid deficiency
C. increased breast size
D. lack of menses

7. Constipation is common in the immediate postpartal period. Factors contributing to the delay of the first stool do NOT include   7.____

    A. decreased fluid intake during labor
    B. increased abdominal tone
    C. decreased intra-abdominal pressure
    D. fear of pain from episiotomy or hemorrhoids

8. In an RH incompatibility, immune globulin must be given within _____ after delivery to effectively destroy fetal antigens before they are able to stimulate the production of permanent maternal antibodies.   8.____

    A. 72 hours   B. 9 days   C. 7 days   D. 2 hours

9. The MINIMUM period for which contraception is recommended for a postpartal woman receiving the rubella vaccine is   9.____

    A. one year   B. two months
    C. six months   D. one week

10. Afterpains are spasmodic uterine contractions that occur during the first few days after delivery to keep the uterus firmly contracted.   10.____
Afterpains are aggravated by all of the following EXCEPT

    A. oxytocin   B. methylergonovine maleate
    C. relaxin   D. breastfeeding

11. Factors contributing to the dizziness and fainting frequently experienced during the early postpartal period include   11.____

    A. dilatation of vessels caused by estrogen
    B. increased intra-abdominal pressure causing splanchnic engorgement
    C. smaller than normal blood loss leading to hypo-volemia
    D. all of the above

12. Postpartum chilling or hypothermic reactions are accompanied by uncontrollable shaking in the early postpartal period.   12.____
The etiology of this effect is not known, but explanations that have been offered include all of the following EXCEPT

    A. nervous and exhaustion responses related to the stress of childbirth
    B. disequilibrium in the internal and external body temperature resulting from waste of muscular exertion
    C. sudden increase of intra-abdominal pressure after delivery
    D. previous maternal sensitization to elements of fetal blood

13. Nursing intervention in a patient with hypothermic or chilling reactions in the postpartal period would NOT include   13.____

A. dry and warm blankets
B. intravenous administration of dentrolene
C. an environment free of drafts
D. warm fluids by mouth

14. When the spinal canal is penetrated, either to inject anesthesia medication or inadvert-   14.____
ently during the effort to place an epidural catheter in a pregnant woman around delivery,
spinal headache is produced.
Nursing intervention in this case includes:
    I.   Avoid straining and coughing
    II. Increase fluid intake
    III. Encourage patient to be in a sitting position for at least six hours after deliv-
         ery
    IV. Reassurance
The CORRECT answer is:

A. I and IV
C. I, II, and IV
B. I, III, and IV
D. II, III, and IV

15. An injection of morphine through the epidural catheter during a cesarean section pro-   15.____
vides the patient with relief of visceral pain during the first few hours.
Its side effects include all of the following EXCEPT

A. respiratory depression
C. urinary frequency
B. nausea and vomiting
D. pruritis

16. Which of the following conditions leads to or predisposes to lacerations or extension of   16.____
episiotomies by laceration?

A. Rapid and uncontrolled delivery
B. Abnormal presentation
C. Instrumental delivery
D. All of the above

17. The goals of nursing management of breastfeeding in the postpartum period include that   17.____
the

A. mother has breastfed as long as she and the baby desire
B. baby's nutritional needs have been met
C. mother verbalizes satisfaction with the experience
D. all of the above

18. Support needs are physical and psychological needs that, if net by the nurse, enhance   18.____
the natural functioning of breastfeeding, prevent problems, facilitate skill development,
and increase maternal confidence.
These needs do NOT necessarily include

A. offering supplementary feedings
B. correct positioning of the baby at the breast
C. early initiation of breastfeeding
D. encouragement of a demand feeding schedule

19. There are a few contraindications to early initiation of breastfeeding, including   19._____

     A.   infant has a 5 min. apgar score under 6
     B.   mother is heavily medicated
     C.   infant is under 36 weeks gestation
     D.   all of the above

20. To position the mother correctly for breastfeeding, a nurse should provide her with the following information: 20._____

     I.   She should place the infant across her abdomen with the head at her antecubital fossa
     II.   Help the woman to adopt an upright, comfortable position
     III.   Her arms may need to be supported by pillows if they are not supported by arms of a chair
     IV.   Grasp the areola behind the nipple

The CORRECT answer is:

     A.   I, II, and III   B.   I, II, and IV
     C.   II, III, and IV   D.   III and IV

21. Information needs are the teaching and learning needs of the mother and her family that, if met, help the mother to care for herself and her infant and to prevent or resolve breastfeeding problems.   21._____

These needs include information regarding

     I.   general knowledge about the breast and the benefits of breastfeeding
     II.   care of the mother, including breast care and diet
     III.   knowledge about whether infant is getting enough milk, understanding the infant's feeding behavior, recognizing growth spurts and normal stool pattern

The CORRECT answer is:

     A.   I and II   B.   I and III
     C.   II and III   D.   I, II, and III

22. Infants on breastfeeding have lower incidences of all of the following EXCEPT   22._____

     A.   Turner's syndrome   B.   dental caries
     C.   allergies and eczema   D.   orthodontic problems

23. Breastfeeding provides many advantages for a mother and her infant, but does NOT provide   23._____

     A.   emotional advantage for mother and infant
     B.   decelerated involution of uterus
     C.   a food composed of over 100 elements different in proportions and chemical composition from equally complex milk of other mammals
     D.   antibodies and other resistant factors that offer protection from infection for the newborn

24. Breast care involves proper hygiene and measures to keep skin in good condition. Effective breast care includes all of the following EXCEPT: 24._____

A. Breasts should be cleansed once a day during daily shower or bath
B. Mother should be taught to air dry her breasts and nipples for 10-15 minutes after each feeding
C. Breasts must be washed before and after each feeding
D. Breast pads without plastic can be used in between feedings to keep the breast dry

25. Despite nursing support and information, problems with breastfeeding can occur, includ-ing   25._____

    A. breast engorgement
    B. colicky baby
    C. sore nipples and mastitis
    D. all of the above

26. Engorgement is a condition in which breasts become very full and firm.   26._____
    General measures to decrease engorgement include all of the following EXCEPT

    A. hot, moist towels or a paper diaper soaked with warm water can be applied to the breast before feeding
    B. completely stop breastfeeding and start with bottle feeding to provide adequate rest
    C. mother should pump her breast every 3 hours if the infant is unable to nurse
    D. a hot shower

27. Sore nipples can be avoided much of the time by proper placement of the infant on the   27._____
    breast.
    Of the following, only _____ is NOT a likely cause of sore nipples.

    A. frequent nursing
    B. reaction from a nipple cream
    C. too much washing of nipples
    D. breast pads that adhere to the nipples or that contain plastic

28. When the infant is slow to gain weight with breastfeeding, frequently offered recommen-   28._____
    dations include

    A. formula supplements
    B. discontinuation of breastfeeding
    C. both of the above
    D. none of the above

29. Although colic is less frequent in the breast-fed infant, it does occur. Its exact cause is not   29._____
    known; therefore, treatment is non-specific.
    Treatment for colic does NOT include

    A. a diet free of cow's milk
    B. large, infrequent feedings
    C. warmth applied to the abdomen to help relieve pain of abdominal cramping
    D. reassurance to the parents

30. If a mother is to breastfeed her infant successfully during periods of separation, she must learn the art of milk expression and storage. 30.____
To effectively pump the breast, the mother should

    A. find a comfortable, relaxing place to sit
    B. stimulate let down by gently stroking or rolling the nipple, massaging the breasts, and thinking about the infant
    C. express milk from one breast until the milk flow slows and then switch to the opposite breast
    D. all of the above

KEY (CORRECT ANSWERS)

1.	B		16.	D
2.	A		17.	D
3.	D		18.	A
4.	C		19.	D
5.	B		20.	C
6.	C		21.	D
7.	B		22.	A
8.	A		23.	B
9.	B		24.	C
10.	C		25.	D
11.	A		26.	B
12.	C		27.	A
13.	B		28.	C
14.	C		29.	B
15.	C		30.	D

TEST 2

DIRECTIONS: Each question or incomplete statement is followed by several suggested answers or completions. Select the one that BEST answers the question or completes the statement. *PRINT THE LETTER OF THE CORRECT ANSWER IN THE SPACE AT THE RIGHT.*

1. To help the mother maintain breastfeeding while working, the nurse should EMPHASIZE   1._____
   that the mother

   A. establish a good milk supply
   B. plan how and where she will pump at work if she is going to supplement with
      breast milk
   C. rest as much as possible
   D. all of the above

2. Preterm breast milk has all of the following nutritionally important substances in higher   2._____
   concentration to help for rapid growth and special developmental needs of the premature
   infant EXCEPT

   A. lipids and proteins   B. lactose
   C. sodium chloride   D. iron

3. Nursing care for the mother of a premature infant who has decided to breastfeed   3._____
   includes

   A. supporting the decision
   B. helping her initiate a milk supply
   C. supporting her when she goes home
   D. all of the above

4. While breastfeeding twins, in the beginning it is advisable to feed them separately, each   4._____
   on a demand schedule, because of the advantages that the

   A. mother's breasts are stimulated frequently
   B. infants are wide awake for feeding
   C. mother gets to know and bond with each twin
   D. all of the above

5. The PRIMARY aims of the postpartum exercise program include restoring   5._____

   A. alignment of the pelvic girdle
   B. function of abdominal and pelvic floor muscle groups
   C. placement of pelvic organs
   D. all of the above

6. Pelvic floor weakness will NOT result in   6._____

   A. possible prolapse of pelvic organs
   B. detraction from normal sexual responses
   C. urinary retention
   D. a weakened low back

7. Pelvic floor contractions caused by exercise of the pelvic floor in turn stimulate circulation and cause which of the following benefits?

    A. Alleviate pain, stiffness, and edema
    B. Encourage return of bladder control
    C. Aid in shrinkage of hemorrhoids
    D. All of the above

7.____

8. To perform diaphragmatic breathing exercises, a woman should adopt all of the following positions EXCEPT

    A. lie supine with knees bent
    B. left hand on the abdomen below the rib cage
    C. right hand turned back and placed on vertebral column
    D. head and knees supported with pillows

8.____

9. The postcesarean new mother presents a dual problem as she has undergone surgery as well as childbirth.
    Of the following, the condition that does NOT distinguish the mother who gives birth by cesarean section is

    A. she becomes fatigued more easily and has more pain
    B. her hospital stay will be shorter
    C. her period of dependency may be prolonged and intense
    D. she may need closer emotional support or counseling

9.____

10. Early ambulation is the key to postcesarean comfort and recovery.
    Gentle, slow ambulation will do all of the following EXCEPT

    A. stimulate circulation, thus reducing stiffness and pain
    B. encourage kidney, bladder, and intestinal activity
    C. eliminate anesthetic agents from her systems more slowly
    D. facilitate healing

10.____

11. Flatus formation is increased following delivery by cesarean section as anesthesia slows bowel action.
    Relief from gas discomfort will NOT be achieved by

    A. lying on right side with right knee drawn down and supported to help open the bowel passage
    B. massaging the abdomen to stimulate peristaltic action
    C. diaphragmatic breathing, pelvic realignment exercises and early ambulation to stimulate bowel activity
    D. a light enema or flush to clear the bowels

11.____

12. Prior to discharge, a nurse should review _____ with the new mother.

    A. diaphragmatic breathing
    B. comfortable positions for resting and feeding as well as alternatives
    C. safety precautions, such as no heavy lifting, no full sit-ups, and no supine double leg lifts
    D. all of the above

12.____

13. With the woman in the dorsal recumbent position, the nurse should examine the legs for color, edema, warmth, symmetry, and varicosities.
The mother should be advised of all of the following interventions that help treat varicose veins EXCEPT:

    A. Avoid clothing that restricts the return of blood flow from the lower extremities
    B. Wear supportive elastic stockings
    C. Elevate the legs
    D. None of the above

13.____

14. Generalized perineal discomfort is a major source of concern to most mothers and becomes a priority for nursing care.
Measures to promote comfort, besides ice packs and sitz baths, include

    A. sitting on a pillow or rubber donut
    B. tightening the buttocks before sitting to avoid pressure on the area
    C. using a local anesthetic spray
    D. all of the above

14.____

15. Behavior of mothering requires the individual to demonstrate those skills and attitudes that are essential to adaptive role performance as a mother.
Possible stimuli that can contribute to ineffective behavior include all of the following EXCEPT

    A. physical condition of the patient, such as long and difficult labor or chronic illness
    B. adequate support systems available to offer physical and emotional security
    C. use of certain medications, such as narcotics
    D. limited knowledge of infant care, increasing the woman's anxiety level regarding the basic skills essential to mothering

15.____

16. With reference to mothering behavior, the final task is to make the transition from the dependent role of patient to the busy and complex world waiting for the mother at home.
The nurse should plan intervention that includes
    I. exploring the availability of support systems to assist the parents in caring for the infant at home
    II. helping the mother and father decide on a plan for division of labor
    III. discouraging the couple from setting aside time for their own activities, as the infant should be their priority
The CORRECT answer is:

    A. I and II
    B. II only
    C. I and III
    D. I, II, and III

16.____

17. Many mothers desire to return home within 24 hours after delivery.
Reasons for preferring early discharge include

    A. facilitation of parent-infant attachment
    B. participation of family and friends in the baby's care
    C. reduction of costs of medical care
    D. all of the above

17.____

18. The American Academy of Pediatrics and the American College of Obstetricians and Gynecologists have developed guidelines for the early discharge of mother and newborn.
All of the following criteria should be met EXCEPT

18.____

A. course of pregnancy has been uncomplicated and should be expected to remain so
B. mother had a vaginal delivery with no evidence of hemorrhage or infection
C. hospitalization has been a minimum of 5 days, during which time the newborn has maintained a stable temperature
D. newborn is at term (38-42 weeks), is of normal weight (2500-4500 g), and is found to be normal by a physician at the discharge examination

19. Expectant parents should be encouraged to attend parent education classes to prepare for the tasks involved in early postpartum and newborn care.
These classes are designed to offer   19._____

A. self-care instructions
B. assistance to parents in understanding the importance of having help at home
C. information about possible equipment that might be needed, such as a breast pump or portable sitz baths, etc.
D. all of the above

20. Of the following newborn factors, only _____ will NOT disturb the normal transition at birth.   20._____

A. meconium aspiration   B. mechanical trauma
C. multiple pregnancies   D. increased lung water

21. All of the following factors stimulate the respiratory center and respirations in the fetus and newborn EXCEPT   21._____

A. cord clamping
B. profound acidosis (pH less than 7.00) or alkalosis (pH greater than 7.50)
C. hypoxemia
D. hypercarbia

22. The one of the following factors that does NOT depress the respiratory center and respiration in the fetus and newborn is   22._____

A. severe cold stress
B. overstretching of alveoli (Hering-Breuer reflex)
C. focal atelactasis
D. maternal narcotics and sedatives

23. The sensory stimuli that are thought to be associated with the initiation of respiration include all of the following EXCEPT   23._____

A. touch   B. darkness   C. sound   D. gravity

24. Mechanical injuries to the fetus involving the eye include   24._____

A. rupture of inner membrane of cornea (descemets)
B. subconjunctival hemorrhage
C. both of the above
D. none of the above

25. The fetus is at greatest risk of severe asphyxia during labor and delivery.   25.____
Maternal _____ is NOT associated with reduction of oxygen transfer.

   A. hyperoxemia   B. hypotension
   C. blood loss   D. hypertension

26. In order for infants to move air in and out of their lungs, they MUST have   26.____

   A. a functioning respiratory center
   B. intact nerves from the brain to the breathing muscles in the chest
   C. a free and clear airway to allow passage of air into and out of lungs
   D. all of the above

27. Primary mechanisms by which the newborn is able to respond to heat loss include which   27.____
of the following?
       I.   Vasomotor control
      II.   Thermal insulation
     III.   Shivering and muscular activity
The CORRECT answer is:

   A. I, II, and III   B. I *only*
   C. I and II   D. III *only*

28. Mechanisms of heat loss in the newborn include   28.____

   A. radiation
   B. conduction
   C. convection and evaporation
   D. all of the above

29. The newborn's increased tendency to lose body heat is related to their   29.____
       I.   limited metabolic capabilities
      II.   small surface area in relation to mass
     III.   decreased thermal insulation
The CORRECT answer is:

   A. I, II, and III   B. I and III
   C. II and III   D. II *only*

30. Principal metabolic disorders that produce seizures in newborns include   30.____
       I.   hypoglycemia
      II.   hypocalcemia
     III.   phenylketonuria
     IV.   hyperoxemia
The CORRECT answer is:

   A. I and III   B. II and IV
   C. I and II   D. II and III

KEY (CORRECT ANSWERS)

1.	D	16.	A
2.	B	17.	D
3.	D	18.	C
4.	D	19.	D
5.	D	20.	C
6.	C	21.	B
7.	D	22.	C
8.	C	23.	B
9.	B	24.	C
10.	C	25.	A
11.	A	26.	D
12.	D	27.	A
13.	D	28.	D
14.	D	29.	B
15.	B	30.	C

EXAMINATION SECTION
TEST 1

DIRECTIONS: Each question or incomplete statement is followed by several suggested answers or completions. Select the one that BEST answers the question or completes the statement. *PRINT THE LETTER OF THE CORRECT ANSWER IN THE SPACE AT THE RIGHT.*

1. In order to accomplish toilet training with a minimum of conflict for the child and the parent, which of these methods by the parent would be BEST?

    A. Put the child on the toilet after breakfast and have him stay there until his bowels move.
    B. Put the child on the toilet and promise him candy when his bowels move.
    C. Disapprove of the child each time he soils himself.
    D. Start toileting the child when he begins fussing about soiling his diapers.

1.____

2. Jennifer, 2 years old, is to receive an antibiotic orally in liquid form.
Before pouring the medication, it is ESSENTIAL for the licensed practical nurse to

    A. wipe the lip of the container with a sterile cotton ball
    B. hold the bottle under warm running water for a few seconds
    C. find out if Jennifer has ever taken a liquid medication
    D. shake the bottle well if there is a precipitate

2.____

3. An 11-year-old boy who is in a spica cast often eats too much and then complains of discomfort.
Which of these measures is likely to be MOST helpful to him concerning this problem?

    A. Give him smaller but more frequent meals
    B. Continue to give him three meals a day, but give him smaller portions
    C. Restrict his fluid intake
    D. Encourage him to eat slowly and to alternate liquids with solids

3.____

Questions 4-9.

DIRECTIONS: Questions 4 through 9 are to be answered on the basis of the following information.

Reggie Dabney, 8 years old, has sickle cell anemia. He is admitted to the hospital in sickle cell crisis.

4. Sickle cell anemia is caused by

    A. genetic factors
    B. antigen-antibody reactions
    C. nutritional deficiencies
    D. metabolic disorders

4.____

5. Reggie complains of pain in his legs and abdomen. Such pain is MOST probably the result of

    A. bleeding into the cellular spaces
    B. clumping of erythrocytes
    C. a generalized infectious process
    D. a shift of intestinal fluid

5.____

6. Reggie is very quiet and lies facing the wall much of the time.
Which of these measures by the licensed practical nurse would be BEST?

    A. Spend time with Reggie other than giving him physical care
    B. Provide Reggie with an opportunity to talk with an older child who also has sickle cell anemia
    C. Assure Reggie at frequent intervals that he is improving
    D. Remind Reggie that being upset might make his condition worse

6.____

7. Mrs. Dabney says to the licensed practical nurse, *I hope Reggie will stop having these crises.*
The nurse's response should be based on which of these understandings?

    A. Sickle cell anemia can be controlled if the disease is diagnosed at birth.
    B. Sickle cell anemia is a chronic disease characterized by periods of crisis through-out life.
    C. If the child with sickle cell anemia is in remission for two years, the disease is con-sidered arrested.
    D. If the child with sickle cell anemia reaches puberty, the crises will no longer occur.

7.____

8. The understanding about children of Reggie's age (8 years) that the licensed practical nurse should keep in mind when planning their play activities is that they

    A. need to have highly structured activities
    B. prefer being with children of the opposite sex
    C. like to be involved with a group of children their own age
    D. usually include an imaginary playmate in their activities

8.____

9. Reggie's condition improves, and plans are made with Mr. and Mrs. Dabney for his dis-charge.
Mrs. Dabney says to the licensed practical nurse, *We're planning to go camping at a lake for the entire summer. It's about four hundred miles from here.*
Because Reggie has sickle cell anemia, which of these suggestions would it be APPROPRIATE for the nurse to make to Mrs. Dabney?

    A. Be sure that Reggie is not exposed to the sun.
    B. Plan to drive for only short periods at a time so that Reggie will have a chance to exercise his legs.
    C. Limit Reggie's fluids while traveling to help prevent him from being carsick.
    D. Ask your physician about the medical facilities that are available where you are going.

9.____

Questions 10-13.

DIRECTIONS: Questions 10 through 13 are to be answered on the basis of the following information.

Reijo Sinisalo, 12 years old, is brought to the emergency room by his parents. A diagnosis of acute appendicitis is made, and Reijo is scheduled for surgery.

An appendectomy is performed. Because the appendix had ruptured, a drain is inserted
in the incision. Reijo is brought to the pediatric unit with an intravenous infusion running. He
has a nasogastric tube connected to intermittent suction.

10.   A nasogastric tube may be inserted for three of the following purposes.   10._____
It would NOT be inserted to

    A.   relieve distension
    B.   re-establish normal peristalsis
    C.   facilitate drainage from the stomach
    D.   allow for the measurement of stomach contents

11.   An antibiotic has been added to Reijo's intravenous fluids.   11._____
The purpose of the antibiotic for Reijo is to

    A.   promote drainage
    B.   facilitate rapid healing
    C.   treat the existing peritonitis
    D.   prevent the development of pneumonia

12.   In the early postoperative period, which of these understandings about administering   12._____
medication for pain to children such as Reijo is ACCURATE?

    A.   Analgesia is usually necessary and is safe if the dosage is calculated for the indi-
vidual child.
    B.   Potential drug addiction should be a major concern in the care of an acutely ill
child.
    C.   Since children are active earlier in the postoperative period than adults, they will
need little or no analgesia.
    D.   Children have a higher tolerance for pain than do adults and, therefore, need
smaller doses of drugs.

13.   Which of these behaviors is characteristic of MOST normal 12-year-olds?   13._____

    A.   Rejection of new routines
    B.   Shyness when meeting new people
    C.   Anxiety caused by separation from parents
    D.   Embarrassment associated with elimination

Questions 14-19.

DIRECTIONS: Questions 14 through 19 are to be answered on the basis of the following information.

Bonnie Tansy, a 3-month-old infant with two siblings, is brought by her mother to the clinic for routine health care. Bonnie has some localized scaling and red areas on her cheeks, neck, and elbows, which are diagnosed as eczema.

14.   Which of these suggestions regarding Bonnie's care is it MOST important for the licensed practical nurse to give Mrs. Tansy?

   A.   Bathe Bonnie daily with a mild soap.
   B.   Keep Bonnie's nails cut short.
   C.   Use only long-sleeved clothing for Bonnie.
   D.   Have the other children in the family avoid contact with Bonnie.

14.____

15.   Which of these behaviors should the licensed practical nurse expect to observe a normal 3-month-old infant doing?

   A.   Holding the bottle during a feeding
   B.   Smiling in response to being talked to
   C.   Turning from the back to the abdomen
   D.   Crying when a stranger approaches

15.____

16.   Bonnie's eczema remains under control until she is 6 months of age. She is then admit-
ted to the hospital because of a severe flare-up of the eczema on her arms and trunk.
Bonnie is wearing elbow restraints.
It would be MOST appropriate to remove her restraints when

   A.   she is being held
   B.   she is sleeping
   C.   she is being wheeled in a carriage around the unit
   D.   the nurse is in her room

16.____

17.   Bonnie is receiving an antihistamine.
The purpose of this medication is to _____ of the lesions.

   A.   promote healing   B.   reducing itching
   C.   limit the spread   D.   prevent infection

17.____

18.   Bonnie is discharged. When she is 1 year old, she is readmitted to the hospital with another flare-up of the eczema.
Which of these recent changes in Bonnie's life is MOST likely related to the increased severity of her eczema?

   A.   A new foam-rubber mattress was placed in her crib.
   B.   Eggs were included in her diet for the first time.
   C.   Her parents had their home air-conditioned.
   D.   She has a new cotton blanket on her bed.

18.____

19.   Bonnie has all of the following abilities.
Which one was probably acquired MOST recently?

   A.   Sitting for extended periods without support
   B.   Transfering a toy from one hand to the other
   C.   Sitting down from a standing position without help
   D.   Rolling over completely

19.____

Questions 20-26.

DIRECTIONS: Questions 20 through 26 are to be answered on the basis of the following information.
Greta Wade, 4 months old, is admitted to the hospital with severe diarrhea and dehydra-
tion. Isolation precautions are instituted. She is to receive nothing by mouth. Mrs. Wade plans
to spend each afternoon with Greta.

20. It would be MOST important to weigh Greta when she is admitted to the unit in order to   20.____

    A.   assess the seriousness of her condition
    B.   determine the presence of edema
    C.   compare her weight with the normal range for her age
    D.   calculate her fluid requirements

21. Greta should received NOTHING by mouth in order to   21.____

    A.   reduce the spread of disease-producing organisms
    B.   provide for a more accurate measurement of stool volume
    C.   prevent aspiration
    D.   decrease activity in the gastrointestinal tract

22. Greta is receiving intravenous fluids.   22.____
Greta's intravenous equipment is to be adjusted so that she receives 18 microdrops
per minute. The licensed practical nurse notices that only 2 microdrops are being delivered per minute.
Before reporting this observation to the nurse in charge, which of these actions should
the nurse take?

    A.   Milk the intraveous tubing
    B.   Check the site of the intravenous infusion
    C.   Open the clamp on the intravenous tubing completely
    D.   Raise the intravenous bottle

23. If Greta's intravenous infusion were to run too fast, which of these complications would   23.____
be MOST likely to occur?

    A.   Severe diarrhea   B.   Thrombus formation
    C.   Renal failure   D.   Circulatory overload

24. Greta's mother, Mrs. Wade, asks the licensed practical nurse what she could do to be   24.____
helpful to Greta. Which of these suggestions should the nurse give to Mrs. Wade?

    A.   Write down the number of stools Greta has.
    B.   Keep track of the fluid in Greta's I.V. bottle.
    C.   Caress Greta frequently when she is awake.
    D.   Remind me when it is time to change Greta's position.

25. Greta's condition improves, and she is started on oral feedings.   25.____
The licensed practical nurse is to feed Greta for the first time.
Which of these measures should be taken in relation to the feeding situation?

    A.   Give Greta a small amount of the feeding at a time.
    B.   Hold Greta in an upright position during the feeding.

    C.   Bubble Greta each time she has taken a half ounce of the feeding.

    D.   Position Greta with her head slightly lower than her chest after feeding her.

26.   Greta is to be weighed daily.   26._____
      At which of these times would it be BEST to weigh her?

    A.   Prior to her first morning feeding

    B.   After she has been bathed

    C.   After her first bowel movement

    D.   Whenever her mother is available to assist with the procedure

Questions 27-32.

DIRECTIONS: Questions 27 through 32 are to be answered on the basis of the following information.

Allen Beam, 20 months old, is to be admitted to the hospital for surgical repair of an
inguinal hernia.

27.   A COMMON symptom of inguinal hernia is   27._____

    A.   protrusion of the umbilicus

    B.   visible peristalsis

    C.   a mass in the groin

    D.   abdominal distension

28.   Allen arrives at the hospital clutching a rather soiled, ragged baby blanket. When his   28._____
      mother attempts to remove the blanket to take it home, Allen cries and holds on to it.
      Which of these comments by the licensed practical nurse would indicate the BEST
      understanding of Allen's needs?

    A.   It looks as if that's Allen's favorite blanket. It's all right for him to keep it with him.

    B.   Let's wait until Allen is involved in an activity, and then I'll take the blanket and give
        it to you next time you come.

    C.   I'll get Allen another blanket. Then he won't mind giving up this one.

    D.   Tell Allen that you only want to take the blanket to wash it and that you'll bring it
        back next time you come.

29.   Allen is to have a venipuncture to obtain a blood specimen. When the physician is ready   29._____
      to take Allen's blood, which of these approaches by the licensed practical nurse would be
      BEST?

    A.   Tell Allen which arm to extend to the physician

    B.   Hold Allen's arm in position for the physician

    C.   Show Allen how to squeeze his fist tight while the needle is being inserted

    D.   Have Allen cover his eyes with one hand while the specimen is being withdrawn

30.   Mrs. Beam tells the licensed practical nurse that she has to leave because she has a 6-   30._____
      month-old baby at home.
      Mrs. Beam says, *Allen has never been away from home without me and I think he's
      going to be very upset.*
      Which of these responses by the nurse would be BEST?

A. Maybe if you promise to bring him his favorite toy when you return, he won't cry so much.
B. If we hear Allen crying, we will send someone in to care for him.
C. I'll stay here with Allen and try to comfort him.
D. Most children only cry for a little while after their mothers leave.

31. Allen is scheduled for surgery and is to have nothing by mouth.
While Allen can have nothing by mouth, he is unhappy and cries for something to drink.
Which of these measures would it be APPROPRIATE to include in his care?

    31.____

A. Taking Allen for a walk
B. Giving Allen chips of ice to suck
C. Having Allen use a pleasant-flavored mouthwash.
D. Explaining to Allen why he cannot have fluids

32. Allen has surgery. He is to be discharged the next day. Mrs. Beam tells the licensed practical nurse that Allen does not drink enough milk.
Which of these foods is the BEST substitute for milk?

    32.____

A. Citrus fruit juice
C. Cheese
B. Cream
D. Root vegetables

Questions 33-40.

DIRECTIONS: Questions 33 through 40 are to be answered on the basis of the following information.

Anna Amorosa, 2 years old, is admitted to the hospital with a diagnosis of laryngotracheobronchitis. She is placed in a Croupette with oxygen.

33. Common symptoms of severe laryngotracheobronchitis include

    33.____

A. swelling of the neck and drooling
B. dyspnea and temperature elevation
C. nausea and vomiting
D. shrill cry and head rolling

34. The licensed practical nurse is unable to count Anna's respirations accurately because she is restless and crying.
Which of these actions by the nurse would be BEST?

    34.____

A. Ask another staff member to count Anna's respirations
B. Record an approximate respiratory rate
C. Postpone taking Anna's respirations until she becomes quiet
D. Average her respirations per minute after taking them for 3 minutes

35. The evening after Anna's admission, Mrs. Amorosa arrives to visit Anna. Mrs. Amorosa says to the licensed practical nurse, *I just put my hand in the tent. Anna's clothing is damp.*
In addition to changing Anna's clothing, which of these actions should the nurse take in response to Mrs. Amorosa's comment?

    35.____

A. Report Mrs. Amorosa's observation to the nurse in charge
B. Encourage Anna to drink fluids to replace those she is losing
C. Take Anna's temperature to compare it with her previous temperature
D. Explain the function of the humidity to Mrs. Amorosa

36. Expected outcomes of oxygen therapy are

    36._____

A. increase in the respiratory and pulse rates
B. increase in the respiratory rate and decrease of the pulse rate
C. decrease of the respiratory rate and increase in the pulse rate
D. decrease of the respiratory and pulse rates

37. Anna's condition improves, and she is to be removed from the Croupette for short periods during the day.
Before returning Anna to the Croupette, the licensed practical nurse should take which of these actions?

    37._____

A. Close the tent and turn on the oxygen flow meter
B. Wipe the inside of the canopy with a disinfectant solution
C. Give Anna fluids to drink
D. Assist Anna in doing deep-breathing exercises

38. Anna's condition has improved. She is ambulatory and is to be discharged soon.
Anna is in the playroom.
Which of these behaviors is typical of a 2-year-old child?

    38._____

A. Playing a simple board game with another child of the same age
B. Sitting quietly with a group of children while listening to a story
C. Coloring within the lines of drawings in a coloring book, using the jumbo-size crayons
D. Engaging in activities near other children but not with them

39. Mrs. Amorosa tells the licensed practical nurse that for the past month Anna has not been eating as much as usual and that she is eating less than her 1-year-old brother.
The MOST likely reason for this change in Anna's appetite is

    39._____

A. dislike of the food she is being given
B. a decrease in her growth rate
C. jealousy of her brother
D. a reluctance to feed herself

40. When Anna is ready for discharge, Mrs. Amorosa asks the licensed practical nurse what she should do if Anna begins to develop symptoms of croup again.
Which of these questions would it be BEST to ask Mrs. Amorosa INITIALLY?

    40._____

A. Has anyone ever showed you how to do postural drainage with Anna?
B. How far from your home is the nearest emergency room?
C. Does rocking Anna or singing to her help to relax her?
D. Does your bathroom steam up easily when you run the hot water?

KEY (CORRECT ANSWERS)

1.	D	11.	C	21.	D	31.	A
2.	D	12.	A	22.	B	32.	C
3.	A	13.	D	23.	D	33.	B
4.	A	14.	B	24.	C	34.	C
5.	B	15.	B	25.	A	35.	D
6.	A	16.	A	26.	A	36.	D
7.	B	17.	B	27.	C	37.	A
8.	C	18.	B	28.	A	38.	D
9.	D	19.	C	29.	B	39.	B
10.	B	20.	D	30.	C	40.	D

BASIC NURSING PROCEDURES:
FUNDAMENTAL NURSING CARE OF THE PATIENT

TABLE OF CONTENTS

BASIC NURSING PROCEDURES:
FUNDAMENTAL NURSING CARE OF THE PATIENT

1. MORNING CARE

PURPOSE

To refresh and prepare patient for breakfast.

EQUIPMENT

Basin of warm water
Towel, washcloth and soap
Toothbrush and dentifrice/mouthwash
Curved basin
Glass of water
Comb

PROCEDURE

1. Clear bedside stand or overbed table for food tray.
2. Offer bedpan and urinal.
3. Wash patient's face and hands.
4. Give oral hygiene.
5. Place patient in a comfortable position for breakfast.
6. Comb hair.

POINTS TO EMPHASIZE

1. Morning care is given before breakfast by night corpsman.
2. Assist handicapped, aged or patients on complete bed rest.

CARE OF EQUIPMENT

Wash, dry and replace equipment.

---

2. ORAL HYGIENE

PURPOSE

To keep mouth clean.
To refresh patient.
To prevent infection and complications in the oral cavity.
To stimulate appetite.

EQUIPMENT

Glass of water
Curved basin
Toothbrush and dentifrice - electric toothbrush if available
Mouth wash
Towel
Drinking tubes as necessary

PROCEDURE

1. A patient who is able to help himself:
    a. Place patient in comfortable position.
    b. Arrange equipment on bedside table within his reach.

2. A patient who needs assistance:
    a. Place patient in comfortable position.
    b. Place towel under his chin and over bedding.
    c. Moisten brush, apply dentifrice and hand to the patient.
    d. Hold curved basin under his chin while he cleanses his teeth and mouth.
    e. Remove basin. Wipe lips and chin with towel.

POINTS TO EMPHASIZE

Oral hygiene is particularly important for patients
    a. who are not taking food and fluid by mouth
    b. with nasogastric tubes
    c. with productive coughs
    d. who are receiving oxygen therapy

CARE OF EQUIPMENT

Wash equipment with soap and hot water, rinse, dry and put away.

———————

3. SPECIAL MOUTH CARE

PURPOSE

To cleanse and refresh mouth.
To prevent infection.

EQUIPMENT

Electric toothbrush if available
Tray with:
Mineral oil or cold cream
Lemon-glycerine applicators
Paper bag
Drinking tubes or straws
Applicators and gauze sponges
Curved basin
Paper wipes
Bulb syringe

Cleansing agents

Tooth paste
Equal parts of hydrogen peroxide and water
Mouthwash

Glass of water
Suction machine for unconscious patient

PROCEDURE

1. Tell patient what you are going to do.
2. Turn patient's head to one side.
3. Brush teeth and gums.
4. When it is not possible to brush teeth and gums, moisten applicator with a cleansing agent and use for cleaning oral cavity and teeth.
5. Assist patient to rinse mouth with water.
6. If patient is unable to use drinking tube, gently irrigate the mouth with a syringe directing the flow of water to side of mouth.
7. Apply lubricant to lips.

For Unconscious Patient

Use suction machine.

4

SPECIAL MOUTH CARE (Continued)

POINTS TO EMPHASIZE
1. Extreme care should be exercised to prevent injury to the gums.
2. Position patient carefully to prevent aspiration of fluids.
3. Caution patient not to swallow mouthwash.

CARE OF EQUIPMENT

Dispose of applicator and soiled gauze. Clean equipment and restock tray.

———————

148

4. CARE OF DENTURES

PURPOSE

To aid in keeping mouth in good condition.
To cleanse the teeth.

EQUIPMENT

Container for dentures
Toothbrush and dentifrice
Glass of water
Mouthwash
Curved basin
Towel
Paper towels

PROCEDURE

1. Have patient rinse mouth with mouthwash.
2. Remove dentures. Place them in container.
3. Have patient brush tongue and gums with mouth-wash.
4. Place a basin under tap in sink and place paper towels in basin. Fill basin with cold water.
5. Hold dentures over basin and under cold running water. Wash with brush and dentifrice.
6. Place dentures in container of cold water. Take to patient's bedside.
7. Replace wet dentures.

POINTS TO EMPHASIZE

1. Handle dentures carefully to prevent breakage.
2. When not in use, dentures should be placed in covered container of cold water and placed in top drawer of locker.
3. Give special attention to the inner surfaces of clips used to hold bridge work or partial plates in place.

CARE OF EQUIPMENT

Wash equipment, rinse, dry and put away.

---

5. BED BATH

PURPOSE

To cleanse the skin.
To stimulate the circulation.
To observe the patient mentally and physically.
To aid in elimination.

EQUIPMENT

Linen and pajamas as required
Half filled basin of water
Bar of soap
Rubbing alcohol/skin lotion
Bedpan and urinal with cover
Bed screens

PROCEDURE

1. Tell patient what you are going to do.
2. Screen patient.
3. Offer bedpan and urinal.
4. Shave patient or allow patient to shave himself.
5. Lower backrest and knee rest if physical condition permits.
6. Loosen top bedding at foot and sides of bed.
7. Remove pillow and place on chair.
8. Remove and fold bedspread and blanket. Place on back of chair.
9. Remove pajamas and place on chair.
10. Assist patient to near side of bed.
11. Bathe the patient:

   a. Eyes:
      (1) Do not use soap.
      (2) Clean from inner to outer corner of eye.

   b. Face, neck and ears.
   c. Far arm.
   d. Place hand in basin and clean nails.
   e. Near arm.
   f. Place hand in basin and clean nails.
   g. Chest.
   h. Abdomen.

BED BATH (Continued)

PROCEDURE (Continued)

12.

    i.   Far leg, foot and nails. Place foot in basin when possible.

    j.   Near leg, foot and nails. Place foot in basin when possible.

    k.   Change water. l. Back and buttocks.

    m.   Genitals and rectal area.

13. Give back rub.
14. Put on pajamas.
15. Comb hair.
16. Make bed.
17. Adjust bed to patient's comfort unless contrain-dicated.

POINTS TO EMPHASIZE

1. Give bed baths daily and P.R.N.
2. Give oral hygiene before bath.
3. Avoid drafts which might cause chilling.
4. Use bath towel under all parts to aid in keeping the bed linen as dry as possible.
5. Change bath water after washing lower extremities and as necessary.
6. Be sure all soap film is rinsed from body to prevent skin irritation.
7. Keep patient well draped at all times.
8. Observe and chart the condition of the skin in regard to lesions, rashes and reddened areas.
9. Pillow should be removed unless contraindicated to give patient a change of position.
10. Assist handicapped patients with shaving.
11. Always move or turn patient toward you.

CARE OF EQUIPMENT

1. Remove soiled linen and place in hamper.
2. Wash equipment, rinse, dry and put away.

6. MAKING AN UNOCCUPIED BED

PURPOSE

To provide a clean, comfortable bed.
To provide a neat appearance to the ward.

EQUIPMENT

Two sheets
Plastic mattress cover
Blanket
Plastic pillow cover
Pillowcase
Protective draw sheet or disposable pads, if indicated

PROCEDURE

1. Place mattress cover on mattress. Where necessary and available, plastic mattress covers are used.
2. Place center fold of sheet in center of bed, narrow hem even with foot of bed.
3. Fold excess sheet under the mattress at head of bed.
4. Miter corner.
   a. Pick up hanging sheet 12 inches from head of bed.
   b. Tuck lower corner under mattress.
   c. Bring triangle down over side of bed.
   d. Tuck sheet under mattress.
5. Pull bottom sheet tight and tuck under side of mattress.
6. If draw sheets are indicated, place in center of bed as illustrated. Tuck excess under mattress.
   a. Linen draw sheet is made by folding a regular bed sheet in half - hem to hem.
7. Place center fold of second sheet in center of bed, with hem even with the top of mattress.
8. Tuck excess under foot of mattress.
9. Center fold blanket in middle of bed 6 inches from top of mattress.
10. Fold excess under foot of mattress.
11. Make mitered corner.

MAKING AN UNOCCUPIED BED (Continued)

PROCEDURE (Continued)

12. Place bedspread on bed, center fold in middle of bed even with the top of the mattress. Fold under blanket.
13. Fold cuff of top sheet over bedspread at head of bed.
14. Tuck excess spread under foot of mattress.
15. Miter corner at foot of mattress.
16. Go to other side of bed and follow steps 3 to 15.
17. Place plastic cover on pillow.
18. Place pillow case on pillow.
19. Place pillow on bed with seams at head of bed, open end away from the entrance to the ward.

POINTS TO EMPHASIZE

1. Woolen blankets are to be used only when cotton blankets are not available.
2. Never use woolen blankets when oxygen therapy is in use.
3. Use protective draw sheet or protective pads when indicated.

———————

MITERED CORNER

Pick up hanging sheet 12 inches from head of bed.

Tuck lower corner under mattress.

Bring triangle down over side of bed.

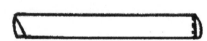

Tuck sheet under mattress.

COMPLETING FOUNDATION
APPLY DRAW SHEETS

1. PLACE RUBBER DRAW SHEET IN CEN-
   TER OF BED

2. TUCK EXCESS RUBBER DRAW SHEET
   IN ON NEAR SIDE OF MATTRESS

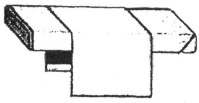

3. PLACE COTTON DRAW SHEET OVER
   RUBBER DRAW SHEET

4. TUCK EXCESS COTTON DRAW SHEET
   IN ON NEAR SIDE OF MATTRESS

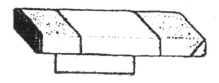

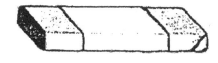

5. TUCK EXCESS RUBBER DRAW SHEET
   IN ON OPPOSITE SIDE OF MATTRESS

6. TUCK EXCESS COTTON DRAW SHEET
   IN ON OPPOSITE SIDE OF MATTRESS

12

7. MAKING AN OCCUPIED BED

PURPOSE

To provide clean linen with least exertion to patient.
To refresh patient.
To prevent pressure sores.

EQUIPMENT

Two sheets
Pillowcase
Blanket
Protective draw sheet or disposable pads, if indicated
Hamper

PROCEDURE

1. Place chair at foot of bed.
2. Push bedside locker away from bed.
3. Pull mattress to head of bed.
4. Loosen all bedding.
5. Remove pillow and place on chair.
6. Remove bedspread by folding from top to bottom, pick up in center and place on back of chair.
7. Remove blanket in same manner.
8. Turn patient to one side of the bed.
9. If cotton draw sheet is used, roll draw sheet close to patient's back.
10. Turn back protective sheet over patient.
11. Roll bottom sheet close to patient's back.
12. Straighten mattress cover as necessary.
13. Place clean sheet on bed with the center fold in the middle and narrow hem even with foot of bed.
14. Tuck in excess at head of bed. Miter corner and tuck in at side.
15. Bring down protective sheet; straighten and tuck in.
16. Make draw sheet by folding a sheet from hem to hem with smooth side out.
17. Place on bed with fold toward head of bed. Tuck in.

MAKING AN OCCUPIED BED (Continued)

PROCEDURE (Continued)

18. Roll patient over to completed side of bed.
19. Go to other side of the bed.
20. Remove soiled sheets and place in hamper.
21. Check soiled linen for personal articles.
22. Turn back draw sheets over patient.
23. Pull bottom sheet tight and smooth.
24. Pull protective sheet and draw sheet tight and smooth.
25. Bring patient to center of bed.
26. Place top sheet over patient, wide hem even with top of mattress.
27. Ask patient to hold clean top sheet.
28. Remove soiled top sheet. Place in hamper.
29. Place blanket 6 inches from top of mattress.
30. Make pleat in sheet and blanket over patient's toes.
31. Tuck in excess at foot of bed and miter corners.
32. Place bedspread on bed even with top of mattress. Fold under blanket.
33. Fold sheet over bedspread and blanket at head of bed.
34. Tuck in excess bedspread at foot of bed. Miter corners. Allow triangle to hang loosely.
35. Put clean pillowcase on pillow. Place under patient's head with closed end toward entrance to ward.
36. Adjust bed as desired by patient.
37. Straighten unit. Leave bedside stand within reach of patient.

POINTS TO EMPHASIZE

1. Always turn patient toward you to prevent possibility of injury and/or falls.
2. Make sure that foundation sheets are smooth and dry.

14

MAKING AN OCCUPIED BED

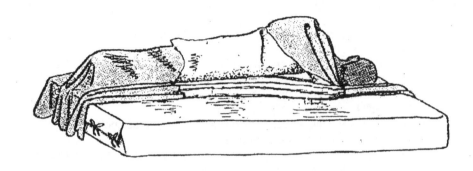

TURN PATIENT TOWARD YOU
FAN FOLD SOILED LINEN
AGAINST PATIENTS BACK

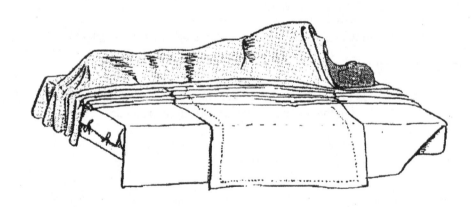

MAKE UP ONE HALF THE BED
BOTTOM SHEET, THEN
RUBBER DRAW SHEET

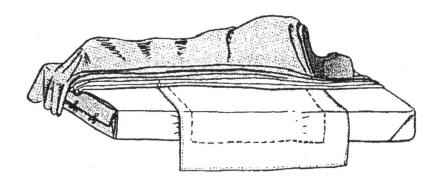

ADD COTTON DRAW SHEET

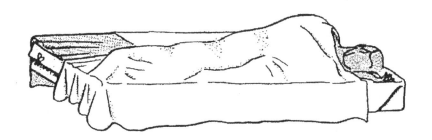

TURN PATIENT ONTO CLEAN LINEN
MAKE OPPOSITE SIDE OF BED

8. SERVING DIETS FROM FOOD CART

PURPOSE

To provide an attractively served food tray for a patient in a hospital where central food tray service is not available.

EQUIPMENT

Cart with food
Cart with trays, dishes, silver, and serving utensils

PROCEDURE

1. Clear the patient's bedside or overbed table.
2. Place table within patient's reach.
3. Place patient in a comfortable position.
4. Wash hands. Wheel food and tray carts to the unit.
5. Place beverage, salad, soup and dessert on the tray.
6. Fill glasses, cups and bowls three fourths full.
7. Serve small portions of hot food in an attractive manner.
8. Check diet list for type of diet each patient is to receive.
9. Carry tray and place it in a convenient position for the patient. Help the patient with the food if necessary.
10. After patient has finished, note how much he has eaten. Collect tray and return to main galley.

POINTS TO EMPHASIZE

1. The ward should be quiet and in readiness for meals.
2. Serve hot food hot and cold food cold.
3. Ice cream, sherbert and jello are kept in the refrigerator until ready to serve.
4. Do not hurry patient.
5. Do not smoke while working with food.
6. Refer to Special Diet Manual for special diet information.
7. Check visible file to determine if patient may have regular diet.
8. Make rounds to check that every patient has been served and received the correct diet.

SERVING DIETS FROM FOOD CART (Continued)

CARE OF EQUIPMENT WHERE MAIN GALLEY DOES NOT HAVE DISH WASHING FACILITIES

1. Scrape and stack dishes:
   a. Solid food into garbage can.
   b. Liquids into drain.
2. Clean and stack trays.
3. Wash dishes with hot soapy water. Stack in dish sterilizer.
4. Follow instructions on sterilizer. Temperature of final rinse water 180° F. Allow to air dry. Put away.
5. Place trays on cart with tray cover, silver and napkins. Salt, pepper, sugar go on all trays except Special Diets.
6. Clean food cart. Return to main galley.

---

9. CENTRAL TRAY SERVICE

PURPOSE

To provide attractively served food to the patient in an efficient manner.

PROCEDURE

1. Check list of patients who are not permitted food or fluids by mouth.
2. Clear bedside or overbed table.
3. Place table within reach of patient.
4. Place patient in comfortable position.
5. Wash hands. Wheel cart with trays to unit.
6. Take tray from cart and check to see if it is complete.
7. Read tray card.
8. See that tray is served to patient listed on the selective menus or the Special Diet Request that is placed on each tray.
9. Call each patient by name or check his identification band. Place his tray within easy reach.
10. Feed patient or assist him as necessary such as buttering his bread, cutting his meat, etc. Allow patient to do as much for himself as possible.
11. Make rounds to check that each patient entitled to a tray has been fed. The Diet List may be used as a check off list.
12. After the patient has finished eating, collect tray immediately and return to cart. Make a note of food eaten and record on Intake and Output Sheet as indicated.
13. Report all complaints about food to Food Service.

POINTS TO EMPHASIZE

1. Serve trays promptly.
2. Do not hurry patient.
3. Make rounds to check that all patients have been fed.

----

10. CARE OF ICE MACHINE AND HANDLING OF ICE, BEDSIDE PITCHERS, AND GLASSES

PURPOSE

To prevent ice machines from becoming a source of infection due to cross-contamination.

EQUIPMENT

To clean and disinfect ice machine:
Clean gloves, disposable
4x4 sponges
Scouring powder
Sodium hypochlorite
Clean 1 gallon container
Clean ice scoop

PROCEDURE

1. Disconnect ice machine from electrical outlet.
2. Wash hands.
3. Use ice scoop to dispose of any existing ice. Pour tap water into ice storage compartment to melt any remaining ice.
4. Put on gloves and remove scale and other debris with 4x4 sponges and scouring powder.
5. Rinse thoroughly with tap water.
6. Place 1/2 ounce of sodium hypocholrite in 1 gallon of water.
7. Using 4 x 4's wipe all accessible areas of interior with sodium hypochlorite solution. Pay particualr attention to ice chute.
8. Repeat step #7.
9. Allow solution to remain in machine for 30 minutes.
10. Rinse thoroughly with clean tap water three times.
11. Clean the exterior of the ice machine.
12. Connect ice machine to electrical outlet.

POINTS TO EMPHASIZE

1. Keep exterior of machine clean between weekly disinfecting of interior.
2. Limit access to ice machine to nursing service personnel.
3. Always keep door closed when not removing ice.
4. Locate ice machine in a "clean" area of the ward or hospital.
5. If ice must be transported, containers should be clean and covered.
6. Use a scoop or tongs when handling ice. Never handle ice with bare hands.
7. Never store the scoop in the ice when not in use.

CARE OF ICE MACHINE AND HANDLING OF
ICE, BEDSIDE PITCHERS, AND GLASSES (Continued)

POINTS TO EMPHASIZE (Continued)

8. The scoop or tongs must be sanitized at least daily.
9. Each patient should have his own bedside water pitcher with cover.
10. Glasses used for drinking water should be sent to the kitchen for exchange of clean glasses on a routine basis.
11. Culture ice machines according to local hospital policy and record in ice culture log.

CARE OF EQUIPMENT

1. Discard disposable equipment.
2. Replace cleaning gear.

11. FEEDING THE HELPLESS PATIENT

PURPOSE

To promote adequate nutrition of the helpless patient.
To encourage self-help when condition permits.

PROCEDURE

1. Place the patient in a sitting position unless otherwise ordered.
2. Place a towel across the patient's chest. Tuck a napkin under his chin.
3. Place tray on overbed table or bedside stand.
4. Give the patient a piece of buttered bread if he is able to hold it.
5. Feed the patient in the order in which he likes to be fed,
6. Offer liquids during the meal. Have patient use a drinking tube if necessary.
7. Give a small amount of food at one time. Allow the patient to chew and swallow food before offering him more. Do not rush your patient.
8. If patient is inclined to talk, talk with him.
9. Note amount of food he has taken. Record amount of fluid if on measured intake and output.
10. Remove tray. Leave patient comfortable.

POINTS TO EMPHASIZE

1. As you are feeding a blind patient tell him what you are offering and whether it is hot or cold.
2. Encourage a blind patient to begin feeding himself as soon as he is able and when indicated.
3. When encouraging a blind patient to feed himself, arrange tray the same way each time. Place foods on plate in the same clockwise direction and fill glasses and cups one-half full to avoid spilling.
4. If patient has difficulty in swallowing, have oral suction machine at bedside.

---

12. EVENING CARE

PURPOSE

To relax and prepare patient for the night.
To observe the patient's condition.

EQUIPMENT

Basin of warm water
Towel, washcloth and soap
Toothbrush, and dentifrice/mouthwash
Curved basin
Glass of water
Rubbing alcohol/skin lotion
Comb

PROCEDURE

1. Offer bedpan and urinal.
2. Give oral hygiene.
3. Wash patient's face and hands.
4. Wash back. Give back rub. Comb hair.
5. Straighten and tighten bottom sheets.
6. Freshen pillows.
7. Place extra blanket at foot of bed if weather is cool.
8. Make provision for ventilation of unit.
9. Clean and straighten unit and remove excess gear.

POINTS TO EMPHASIZE

1. Indicated for all bed patients and those on limited activity.
2. Change soiled linen as necessary.
3. Patient may assist with care as condition permits.
4. Ask the patient if soap may be used on the face.
5. Screen patients who require the use of bedpan.

---

13. CARE OF THE SERIOUSLY ILL PATIENT

PURPOSE

To provide optimum care and close observation of the seriously ill patient.
To keep the patient mentally and physically comfortable.

EQUIPMENT

Special mouth care tray
Rubbing alcohol/skin lotion
Bed linen as necessary
Pillow and/or supporting appliances
Special equipment as needed:

I.V. Standard
Suction machine
Oxygen
Drainage bottles
Intake and Output work sheet

PROCEDURE

1. Place patient where he can be easily and <u>closely</u> observed.
2. Keep room quiet, clean and clear of excess gear.
3. Bathe patient daily and P.R.N.
4. Maintain good oral hygiene every 2-4 hours.
5. Wash, rub back and change position every 2 hours unless contraindicated.
6. Speak to patient in a calm, natural tone of voice even if he appears to be unconscious.
7. Report any sudden change in condition.
8. Keep an accurate intake and output record if ordered.
9. Offer fluids if patient is conscious and is able to take them.
10. Record and Report:
    a. Changes in T.P.R. and blood pressure.
    b. State of consciousness.
    c. All observations.

CARE OF THE SERIOUSLY ILL PATIENT (Continued)

POINTS TO EMPHASIZE

1. All patients are seen by a chaplain when they are placed on the Serious or Very Seriously ill list.
2. Be considerate and kind to the patient's relatives.
3. Keep charting up-to-date.
4. Do not discuss patient's condition when the conversation might be overheard by the patient or unauthorized persons.
5. Refer all questions concerning the patient's condition to the doctor or nurse.
6. Be sure all procedures for placing a patient on the SL or VSL have been completed; for exmaple, inventory of personal effects and valuables.

———

COMMON DIAGNOSTIC NORMS

CONTENTS

COMMON DIAGNOSTIC NORMS

1. RESPIRATION: From 16-20 per minute.

2. PULSE-RATE: Men, about 72 per minute.
   Women, about 80 per minute.

3. BLOOD PRESSURE:
   Men: 110-135 (Systolic)   Women: 95-125   (Systolic)
           70-85 (Diastolic)   65-70   (Diastolic)

4. BASAL METABOLISM: Represents the body energy expended to maintain respiration, circulation, etc. Normal rate ranges from plus 10 to minus 10.

5. BLOOD:

   a. Red Blood (Erythrocyte) Count:
   Male adult - 5,000,000 per cu. mm.
   Female adult - 4,500,000 per cu. mm.
      (Increased in polycythemia vera, poisoning by carbon monoxide, in chronic pulmonary artery sclerosis, and in concentration of blood by sweating, vomiting, or diarrhea.)
      (Decreased in pernicious anemia, secondary anemia, and hypochronic anemia.)
   b. White Blood (Leukocyte) Count: 6,000 to 8,000 per cu. mm.
      (Increased with muscular exercise, acute infections, intestinal obstruction, coronary thrombosis, leukemias.)
      (Decreased due to injury to source of blood formation and interference in delivery of cells to bloodstream, typhoid, pernicious anemia, arsenic and benzol poisoning.)
      The total leukocyte group is made up of a number of diverse varieties of white blood cells. Not only the total leukocyte count, but also the relative count of the diverse varieties, is an important aid to diagnosis. In normal blood, from:
      70-72% of the leukocytes are *polymorphonuclear neuirophils.*
      2-4% of the leukocytes are *polymorphonuclear eosinophils.*
      0-.5% of the leukocytes are *basophils,*
      20-25% of the leukocytes are *lymphocytes.*
      2-6% of the leukocytes are *monocytes.*
   c. Blood Platelet (Thrombocyte) Count:
      250,000 per cu. mm. Blood platelets are important in blood coagulation.

   d. Hemoglobin Content:
      May normally vary from 85-100%. A 100% hemoglobin content is equivalent to the presence of 15.6 grams of hemoglobin in 100 c.c. of blood.
   e. Color Index:
      Represents the relative amount of hemoglobin contained in a red blood corpuscle compared with that of a normal individual of the patient's age and sex.
      The normal is 1. To determine the color index, the percentage of hemoglobin is divided by the ratio of red cells in the patient's blood to a norm of 5,000,000.
      Thus, a hemoglobin content of 60% and a red cell count of 4,000,000 (80% of 5,000,000) produces an abnormal color index of .75.

f. Sedimentation Rate:

Represents the measurement of the speed with which red cells settle toward the bottom of a containing vessel. The rate is expressed in millimeters per hour, and indicates the total sedimentation of red blood cells at the end of 60 minutes.

Average rate:	4-7 mm. in 1 hour
Slightly abnormal rate:	8-15 mm. in 1 hour
Moderately abnormal rate:	16-40 mm. in 1 hour
Considerably abnormal rate:	41-80 mm. in 1 hour

(The sedimentation rate is above normal in patients with chronic infections, or in whom there is a disease process involving destruction of tissue, such as coronary thrombosis, etc.)

g. Blood Sugar:

90-120 mg. per 100 c.c. (Normal)

In mild diabetics: 150-300 mg. per 100 c.c.

In severe diabetics: 300-1200 mg. per 100 c.c.

h. Blood Lead:

0.1 mg. or less in 100 c.c. (Normal). Greatly increased in lead poisoning.

i. Non-Protein Nitrogen:

Since the function of the kidneys is to remove from the blood certain of the waste products of cellular activity, any degree of accumulation of these waste products in the blood is a measure of renal malfunction. For testing purposes, the substances chosen for measurement are the nitrogen-containing products of protein combustion, their amounts being estimated in terms of the nitrogen they contain. These substances are urea, uric acid, and creatinine, the sum total of which, in addition to any traces of other waste products, being designated as total non-protein nitrogen (NPN).

The normal limits of NPN in 100 c.c. of blood range from 25-40 mg. Of this total, urea nitrogen normally constitutes 12-15 mg., uric acid 2-4 mg., and creatinine 1-2 mg.

6. URINE:

a. Urine - Lead:

0.08 mg. per liter of urine (normal).

(Increased in lead poisoning.)

b. Sugar:

From none to a faint trace (normal).

From 0.5% upwards (abnormal).

(Increased in diabetes mellitus.)

c. Urea:

Normal excretion ranges from 15-40 grams in 24 hours.

(Increased in fever and toxic states.)

d. Uric Acid:

Normal excretion is variable. (Increased in leukemia and gout.)

e. Albumin:

Normal renal cells allow a trace of albumin to pass into the urine, but this trace is so minute that it cannot be detected by ordinary tests.

f. Casts:
In some abnormal conditions, the kidney tubules become lined with substances which harden and form a mould or *oast* inside the tubes. These are later washed out by the urine, and may be detected microscopically. They are named either from the substance composing them, or from their appearance. Thus, there are pus casts, epithelial casts from the walls of the tubes, hyaline casts formed from coagulable elements of the blood, etc.

g. Pus Cells:
These are found in the urine in cases of nephritis or other inflammatory conditions of the urinary tract.

h. Epithelial Cells:
These are always present in the urine. Their number is greatly multiplied, however, in inflammatory conditions of the urinary tract.

i. Specific Gravity:
This is the ratio between the weight of a given volume of urine to that of the same volume of water. A normal reading ranges from 1.015 to 1.025. A high specific gravity usually occurs in diabetes mellitus. A low specific gravity is associated with a polyuria.

7. SPINAL FLUID:

a. Spinal Fluid Pressure (Manometric Reading):
100-200 mm. of water or 7-15 mm, of mercury (normal).
(Increased in cerebral edema, cerebral hemorrhage, meningitis, certain brain tumors, or if there is some process blocking the fluid circulation in the spinal column, such as a tumor or herniated nucleus pulposus impinging on the spinal canal.)

b. Quickenstedt's Sign:
When the veins in the neck are compressed on one or both sides, there is a rapid rise in the pressure of the cerebrospinal fluid of healthy persons, and this rise quickly disappears when pressure is removed from the neck. But when there is a block of the vertebral canal, the pressure of the cerebrospinal fluid is little or not at all affected by this maneuver.

c. Cerebrospinal Sugar:
50-60 mg. per 100 c.c. of spinal fluid (normal).
(Increased in epidemic encephalitis, diabetes mellitus, and increased intracranial pressure.)
(Decreased in purulent and tuberculous meningitis.)

d. Cerebrospinal Protein:
15-40 mg. per 100 c.c. of spinal fluid (normal).
(Increased in suppurative meningitis, epileptic seizures, cerebrospinal syphilis, anterior poliomyelitis, brain abscess, and brain tumor.)

e. Colloidal Gold Test:
This test is made to determine the presence of cerebrospinal protein.

f. Cerebrospinal Cell Count:
0-10 lymphocytes per cu. mm. (normal).

g. Cerebrospinal Globulin:
Normally negative. It is positive in various types of meningitis, various types of syphilis of the central nervous system, in poliomyelitis, in brain tumor, and in intracranial hemorrhage.

8. SNELLEN CHART FRACTIONS AS SCHEDULE LOSS DETERMINANTS:

    a. Visual acuity is expressed by a Snell Fraction, where the numerator represents the distance, in feet, between the subject and the test chart, and the denominator represents the distance, in feet, at which a normal eye could read a type size which the abnormal eye can read only at 20 feet.

    b. Thus, 20/20 means that an individual placed 20 feet from the test chart clearly sees the size of type that one with normal vision should see at that distance.

    c. 20/60 means that an individual placed 20 feet from the test chart can read only a type size, at a distance of 20 feet, which one of normal vision could read at 60 feet.

    d. Reduction of a Snellen Fraction to its simplest form roughly indicates the amount of vision remaining in an eye. Thus, a visual acuity of 20/60 corrected implies a useful vision of 1/3 or 33 1/3%, and a visual loss of 2/3 or 66 2/3% of the eye.

Similarly:

Visual Acuity (Corrected)	Percentage Loss of Use of Eye
20/20	No loss
20/25	20%
20/30	33 1/3%
20/40	50%
20/50	60%
20/60	66 2/3%
20/70	70% (app.)
20/80	75%
20/100	100% (since loss of 80% or more constitutes industrial blindness)

GLOSSARY OF MEDICAL TERMS

CONTENTS

GLOSSARY OF MEDICAL TERMS

A

Abduction
Movement of limb away from middle line of the body.

Abrasion
A scraping away of a portion of the skin.

Abscess
Localized collection of pus or matter.

Acetabulum
Cup-shaped depression on external surface of the pelvic bone (innominate) into which the head of femur, or thighbone, fits.

Achilles Reflex
Movement of foot downward when the tendon immediately above the heel bone is struck.

Acromion
Process of bone constituting tip of shoulder.

Adduction
Movement of limb toward middle line of body.

Adhesion
The matting together of two surfaces by inflammation.

Alae Nash
Outer flaring walls of the nostrils.

Allergic
Reaction of tissues of the body to a protein substance to which the body is especially sensitive.

Anemia
A condition in which the red blood cells and/or hemoglobin are reduced.

Aneurysm
Sac, filled with blood, formed by the local dilation of walls of artery.

Angina Pectoris
Pain in chest associated with heart disease.

Ankyloses
Complete absence of motion at a joint.

Anterior
The anatomical "front" of the body.

Aorta
Main trunk of the systemic arterial system, arising from base of left ventricle.

Apex
Extremity of conical or pyramidal structure, such as heart or lung.

Aphasia
Loss of power of speech by damage to speech center.

Apoplexy
Another word for stroke.

Arrhythmia
Loss of normal rhythm of the heart.

Arteriosclerosis
Hardening of the arteries.

Artery
> Blood vessel conveying blood away from the heart to different parts of the body.

Arthritis
> Inflammation of a joint.

Arthrodesis
> Stiffening of a joint.

Articulation
> Joint.

Asbestosis
> Dust disease of asbestos workers.

Aseptic
> Free of germs.

Aspiration
> Withdrawal, by suction, of air or fluid from any cavity.

Asthma
> Disease marked by recurrent attacks of shortness, of breath, due to temporary change in bronchial tubes, making person uncomfortable.

Astigmatism
> An abnormality in the curve of the 'anterior visual surface of the eyeball.

Astragalus
> One of the ankle bones.

Ataxia
> Disturbance of coordination of muscular movements.

Atelectasis
> Collapse of lung tissue due to failure of entrance of air into air-cells.

Atrophy
> Wasting or diminution in size of a structure.

Audiogram
> Graphic record made by an audiometer, an electrical instrument for recording acuity of hearing.

Auricular fibrillation
> Irregular beat as to time and force beginning in auricle of the heart.

Auscultation
> The act of listening to sounds within the body.

Axillary
> Relating to armpit.

B

Baker's Cyst
> Enlargement of synovial sac in the back of the knee joint.

Basal Metabolism
> The energy expended for the absolute minimum requirements of the body at complete rest.

Bell's Palsy
> A form of facial paralysis.

Benign
> Not malignant.

Biceps Muscle
> A muscle over front of arm.

Bifida

Split or cleft.

Bilateral

Relating to or having two sides.

Blood Pressure

Pressure or tension of the blood within the arteries.

Brachial

Pertaining to the arm.

Bradycardia

Abnormal slowness of the heartbeat.

Brain

Mass of nerve tissue which is contained within the skull.

Bronchiectasis

Dilation of the narrowest portions of the breathing tubes of the lung.

Bronchitis

Inflammation of mucus membrane of bronchial tubes.

Buerger's Disease

Thromboangiitis obliterans; obliteration and inflammation of the larger arteries and veins of a limb by clotting and inflammation, involving nerve trunks.

Bursa

A lubricating sac usually found at pressure points or around joints.

Bursitis

Inflammation of the bursa.

C

Calcaneum

The os calcis, or heel bone.

Calcification

X-ray opaque substance found in serious tissues of the body.

Canthus

Either extremity of the slit between the eyelids.

Capitellum

Portion of bone found at the end of the arm bone.

Capsule

Fibrous membrane which envelopes an organ, joint or a foreign body.

Carbuncle

Group of boils resulting in localized gangrene or death of affected tissues.

Cardiac

Pertaining to the heart.

Cardiologist

Heart specialist.

Catheter

Hollow cylinder of silver, India rubber or other material, designed to be passed into a hollow area for drainage purposes.

Cartilage

White substance which covers ends of bones.

Causalgia

A painful condition.

Cellulitis

Diffuse inflammation of cellular tissue, i.e., especially loose cellular tissue just underneath skin.

Cephalalgia

Headache.

Cerebellum

Back part of the brain, concerned in coordination of movements.

Cerebrum

Front part of the brain, concerned with the conscious processes of the mind.

Cervix

Neck or neck-like part.

Charcot's joint

Painless joint destruction.

Cholecystectomy

Surgical removal of the gall-bladder.

Cholecystis

Inflammation of gall-bladder.

Cholelithiasis

Gallstone.

Chorio-Retinal

Relating to the visual tissue of eye and its supporting structure.

Chondral

Pertaining to cartilage.

Cicatrix

Scar.

Cirrhosis

Fibrosis or sclerosis of any organ; hardening.

Clavicle

Collar bone.

Clonus

Muscular spasm in which contraction and relaxation of muscle follow one another in rapid succession.

Coccydynia

Pain in the coccyx.

Coccygectomy

Removal of the coccyx.

Coccygeal

Relating to the coccyx.

Coccyx

Small bone at the end of the spinal column in man.

Congenital

Existing at birth.

Congestion

Engorgement of blood vessels of a part.

Conjunctiva

Delicate membrane which lines the inner surface of the eyelids and covers the eyeball in front.

Colles Fracture

Fracture of lower end of radius

Colon

The last part of the intestinal tract.

Comminuted

Broken into more than two fragments.

Concussion

Injury of a soft structure, as the brain, resulting from a blow or violent shaking.

Coronary Artery

The artery providing nutrition to the heart muscle.

Cornea

Transparent structure forming the anterior part of the external layer of eyeball.

Cortex

Outer portion of an organ, such as the kidney, as distinguished from inner or medullary portion; external layer of gray matter covering hemispheres of cerebrum and cerebellum.

Costal

Pertaining to the ribs.

Coxa

Hip joint.

Cranium

Skull.

Crepitus

Abnormal sounds heard in the case of fractured bones and diseased tissues when rubbing together.

Curettage

Scraping the interior of a cavity for the removal of tissue.

Cutaneous

Relating to the skin.

Cyanosis

Blueish discoloration of external tissue, e.g. lips, nails, skin.

Cyst

Abnormal sac which contains a liquid or semi-solid.

Cystoscopy

Inspection of the interior of the bladder with a cystoscope.

Cystostomy

Formation of a more or less permanent opening into the urinary bladder.

D

Dactyl

Digit: Finger or toe.

Decompensation

Failure to maintain normal function as in heart failure.

Deltoid

Triangular-shaped muscle of the shoulder.

Dementia

Form of insanity.

Dermatitis

Inflammation of the skin.

Dermatologist

Skin specialist.

Dermaphytosis

Skin disease due to presence of a vegetable microparasite.

Desiccation

The removal of tissue by chemical, physical, electrical, freezing, or x-ray.

Diabetes (Melitus)

A disease having symptoms of excessive urine and sugar excretion.

Diaphragm

Muscular partition between thorax and abdomen.

Diarrhea

Abnormally frequent discharge of fluid fecal matter from the bowel.

Diastasis

Simple separation of normally joined parts.

Diastole

Period of rest during which heart is filling up for next beat.

Diathermy

Local elevation of temperature in tissues, produced by special form of high-frequency current.

Diathesis

Predisposition to a disease.

Digit

Finger or toe.

Dilatation

Enlargement, due to stretching or thinning out of tissues.

Diplopia

Double-vision.

Disc

A round flat surface variously found in eye and spinal column conditions.

Dislocation

Most frequently used in orthopedics to describe a disturbance of normal relationship of bones which enter into formation of a joint.

Distal

Farthest from the point of origin; the term is usually used in connection with the extremities.

Diverticulum

Pouch or sac opening out from a tubular organ.

Dorsal

Relating to the back; posterior.

Dorsum

The back; upper or posterior surface or back of any part.

Duct

Tube or passage with well-defined walls for passing excretions or secretions.

Duodenum

Upper portion of intestinal tube connecting with stomach.

Dupuytren's Contraction

Contraction of the palmar fascia causing permanent flexion of one or more fingers.

Dura Mater

Outermost and toughest of three membranes covering brain and spinal cord.

Dysphagia

Difficulty in swallowing.

Dyspnoea

Difficulty in breathing.

Dysuria

Difficulty or pain in urination.

E

Ecchymosis

Black and blue spot on the skin.

Ectropion

A rolling outward of the margin of an eyelid.

Eczema

A form of dermatitis.

Edema

Swelling due to watery effusion in the intercellular spaces.

Electrocardiogram

Graph of electric currents in the heart.

Electrocardiograph

Instrument for producing electrocardiogram.

Embolus

Clot or plug brought by blood-current from distant part.

Embolism

The plugging up of a blood vessel by a floating mass.

Eminence

Circumscribed area raised above general area of surrounding surface.

Emphysema

Abnormal distention with loss of elasticity of the air sacs of the lung.

Empyema

Accumulation of pus or matter in normally closed cavity on the surface of the lung.

Encephalitis

Inflammation of the brain substance.

Encephalogram

Roentgenogram of contents of the skull.

Encephalopathy

Conditions of disease of the brain.

Endocrine Gland

A gland which furnishes internal secretion.

Endogenous

Originating or produced within organism or one of its parts.

Enophthalmos

Recession of the eyeball within the orbit.

Epicardium

Cover of the heart.

Epicondyle

Projection from long bone near articular extremity above or upon condyle.

Epidermis

Outermost layer of the skin.

Epididymis

Oblong or boat-shaped body located on back of testicle.

Epidural

Upon the outer envelope of the brain.

Epigastric

Depression at pit of abdominal wall at tip of sword-shaped cartilage of sternum.

Epilepsy, Jacksonian
Convulsive contractions affecting localized groups of muscles without disturbance of mentality.

Epiphysis
Ends of long bones.

Epistaxis
Bloody nose.

Epithelium
Covering of skin and mucus membrane consisting of epithelial cells.

Epithelioma
Cancer of the skin or mucus membrane.

Erector spinae
Muscle keeping the spine erects.

Eruption
A breaking out; redness, spotting or other visible phenomena on the skin or mucus membrane.

Erythema
Abnormal redness of the skin.

Esophagus
Gullet. Tube connecting mouth to stomach.

Etiology
Cause.

Eversion
A turning outward, as of the eyelid or foot.

Exacerbation
Increase in severity of disease or symptoms.

Excision
Operative removal of a portion of an organ.

Excrescence
Outgrowth from the surface, especially a pathological growth.

Exogenous
Originating or produced outside.

Exophthalmus
Protrusion or prominence of the eyeball.

Exostosis
Bony tumor springing from surface of a bone, most commonly seen at muscular attachments.

Extensor
A muscle the contraction of which tends to straighten a limb.

Extrasystole
Premature contraction of one or more heart chambers.

Exudate
A fluid, often coagulable, extravasated into tissue or cavity.

F

Facies
Face, countenance, expression; surface.

Fascia
Sheet or band of fibrous tissue.

Felon

Abscess in terminal phalanx of a finger.

Femoral

Relating to the femur or thigh.

Femur

Thigh bone.

Fibrillation

Totally irregular beat.

Fibroma

Fibroid tumor.

Fibrosis

Pathological formation of fibrous tissue.

Fibula

Smaller calf bone.

Fistula

Abnormal passageway leading to surface of body.

Flexion

Bending of a joint.

Flexor

A muscle the action of which is to flex a joint.

Follicle

Very small excretory or secretory sac or gland.

Foramen

Aperture through a bone or membranous structure.

Fracture, Comminuted

Bone broken into more than two pieces.

Fracture, Ununited

One in which union fails to occur.

Frontal

Relating to the front of body.

Fundus

Base of a hollow organ.

Fusiform

Spindle-shaped, tapering at both ends.

G

Ganglion

Usually used to describe a cystic tumor occurring on a tendon sheath or in connection with a joint.

Gangrene

Death or masse of any part of the body.

Gastric

Pertaining to the stomach.

Gastrocnemius

One of the calf muscles.

Genitalia

Organs of reproduction.

Genito-Urinary

Relation to reproduction and urination, noting organs concerned.

Genu

Knee

Genu-Valgum

Knock-knee.

Gladiolus

Middle and largest division of sternum (chest bone).

Gland

Secreting organ.

Glaucoma

Increased pressure in the eyeball.

Gluteal

Pertaining to the buttocks.

Greenstick Fracture

Incomplete fracture.

Gynecologist

Specialist in the treatment of diseases peculiar to women.

H

Hallux

Great toe.

Hallux valgus

Deviation of great toe toward inner or lateral side of the foot (bunion).

Haematemesis

Vomiting of blood.

Haemoglobin

Coloring matter of blood in red blood corpuscles.

Haemoptysis

Discharge of blood from the lungs by coughing.

Hemarthrosis

Effusion of blood into cavity of a joint.

Hematoma

Swelling formed by effused blood.

Hematuria

Passage of blood in the urine.

Hemianopsia

Loss of vision for one-half of visual field.

Hemorrhage

Bleeding, especially if profuse.

Hemorrhoids

Piles, a varicose condition causing painful swellings of the anus.

Hepatic

Pertaining to the liver.

Herania

Protrusion of organ outside of its normal confines.

Hernioplasty

Operation for hernia.

Herniotomy

Operation for relief of hernia.

Humerus

Bone of the upper arm.

Hydrarthrosis

Effusion of a serous fluid into a joint cavity.

Hydrocele

Circumscribed collection of fluid around the testicle.

Hydrone Phrosis

Dilatation inside kidney due to obstruction of flow of urine.

Hyperaesthesia

Excessive sensitiveness of the skin to touch or hypersensitiveness of any special sense.

Hyperglycaemia

Abnormally large proportion of sugar in blood.

Hypertension

High blood pressure often associated with arteriosclerosis.

Hyperthrophy

Enlargement, general increase in bulk of a part or organ, not due to tumor formation.

Hypogastrium

Lower middle region of the abdomen.

Hypoplasia

Under-development of structure.

Hypothenar

Fleshy mass at the inner (little finger) side of the palm.

Hysteria

A functional nervous condition characterized by lack of emotional control and sudden temporary attacks of mental, emotional or physical aberration.

I

Ileum

Portion of the small intestine.

Ilium

One of the bones of the pelvis.

Impacted

Driven in firmly.

Incontinence

Inability to retain a natural discharge.

Induration

Hardening; spot or area of hardened tissue

Infarct

Death of tissue due to lack of blood supply

Inguinal

Relating to the groin.

In situ

In position.

Intercostal

Between the ribs

Interstitial

Relating to spaces within any structure.

Intertrochanteric

Between the two trochanters of the femur or thigh bone

Intervertebral
> Between two vertebrae.

Iris
> Circular colored portion of the eye which surrounds pupil

Ischaemia
> Local and temporary deficiency of blood.

Ischium
> One of the pelvic bones.

J

Jaundice
> Yellowness of tissues due to absorption of bile.

Jejunum
> Portion of small intestine about 8 feet long, between duodenum and ileum.

K

Kienboeck Disease
> Increased porosity and softness of certain carpal bones.

Keloid
> Peculiar overgrowth of hyaline connective tissues in the skin of predisposed individuals after injury or scarring.

Keratitis
> Inflammation of the cornea.

Kyphosis
> Curvature of the spine, hump-back, hunch-back.

L

Laceration
> Separation of tissue (cut).

Lacriminal
> Relating to the tears apparatus.

Laminae
> Flattened portions of the sides of a vertebral arch.

Laminectomy
> Removal of one or more laminae from the vertebrae.

Larynx
> Organ of voice production.

Lesion
> Any hurt, wound or degeneration.

Leucocytosis
> Temporary increase in relative number of white blood cells in the blood.

Leucopenia

Abnormal decrease in number of white blood corpuscles.

Ligament

Tough fibrous band which connects one bone with another.

Lipoma

Tumor composed of fatty tissue.

Lordosis

Anteroposterior curvature of the spine (opposite to kyphosis).

Lue tic

Syphilitic.

Lumbar

Lower back.

Lumbar Vertebrae

The five vertebrae between the thoracic vertebrae and the sacrum.

Luxation

Dislocation.

Lymphangitis

Inflammation of the lymphatic vessels.

M

Malar

Relating to the cheek-bone.

Malignant

Resistant to treatment; occurring in severe form; tending to grow worse and (in the case of a tumor) to recur after removal. Usually indicates poor end result.

Malleoli

Rounded bony prominences on both sides of the ankle joint.

Mandible

Lower jaw.

Manubrium

Upper portion of the sternum.

Mastectomy

Amputation of the breast.

Maxilla

Upper jaw.

Meatus

Passage or opening.

Meninges

Membranes, specifically the envelope of brain and spinal cord.

Meningitis

Inflammation of the meninges.

Meniscus

Intraarticular fibrocartilage of crescentic or discoid shape found in certain joints.

Mesentery

Web or membrane connecting bowel tube to posterior abdominal wall (a portion of the peritoneum).

Metabolism

The total operation of building up and breaking down tissues.

Metacarpus

Part of hand between wrist and fingers; palm; five metacarpal bones collectively which form skeleton of this part.

Metastasis

Transfer of disease, usually malignant, to remote part of the body.

Metatarsalgia

Pain in the region of the metatarsus(or ball of foot).

Metatarsus

Anterior portion of foot between instep and toes, having as its skeleton five long bones articulating anteriorly with the phalanges.

Mottling

Spotting with patches of varying shades of colors.

Mucocutaneous

Relating to mucus membrane and skin, noting the line of junction of the two at the nasal, oral, vaginal and anal orifices.

Musculature

Arrangement of muscles in a part or in the body as a whole.

Myalgia

Muscular pain.

Myelitis

Inflammation of the substance of the spinal cord.

Myelograph

X-ray picture of spinal cord using radio-opaque substance.

Myocardium

Heart Muscle.

Myocarditis

Inflammation of the muscular walls of the heart.

Myositis

Inflammation of a muscle.

N

Navicular

Boat-shaped, noting a bone in the wrist and one in the ankle.

Nausea

Sickness at the stomach; inclination to vomit.

Nephritis

Inflammation of the kidney.

Necrosis

Death en masse of a portion of tissue.

Nephrosis

Non-inflammatory disease of the kidney.

Neuralgia

Pain radiating along a nerve.

Neuritis

Inflammation of a nerve.

Neurologist

Nerve specialist.

Neuroma

Tumor made up largely of nerve tissue.

Neuropsychiatric
Relating to disease of both mind and nervous system.

Neurosis
Functional derangement of the nervous system.

Nocturia
Bed-wetting.

Node
Knob; circumscribed swelling; circumscribed mass of differentiated tissue; knuckle.

Nucleus Pulposus
Gelatinous center of an intervertebral disc.

Nystagmus
Continuous movement of the eyeballs in the horizontal or vertical plains.

O

Occipital
Relating to the back of the head.

Occlude
To close up or fit together.

Occular
Relating to the eye; visual.

Occult
Hidden; concealed, noting a concealed hemorrhage, the blood being so changed as not to be readily recognized.

Olecranon
Tip of the elbow.

Omentum
Web or apron-like membranous structure lying in front of the intestines.

Opacities
Areas lacking in transparency.

Opthalmia
Disease of the eye.

Opthalmologist
Specialist in eye diseases and refractive errors of the eye.

Optic
Relating to the eye or to vision.

Optometrist
Person without medical training who fits glasses to correct visual defects.

Orbit
Eye- socket.

Orchitis
Inflammation of the testicle.

Orchidectomy
Castration; removal of one or both testicles.

Orthopedics
Branch of surgery which has to do with treatment of diseases of joints and spine and correction of deformities.

Orthopnea
Ability to breathe with comfort only when sitting erect or standing.

Os
> Bone

Oscalcis
> Heel-bone.

Ossification
> Formation of bone; change into bone.

Osteoma
> Bone tumor.

Osteomyelitis
> Inflammation of bone and bone marrow.

Osteoporosis
> Disease of bone marked by increased porosity and softness ("thinning" of bone).

Osteotomy
> Cutting a bone, usually by saw or chisel, for removal of a piece of dead bone, correction of knock-knee or other deformity, or for any purpose whatsoever.

Otologist
> Specialist in diseases of the ear.

P

Paget's Disease
> Usually refers to a bone disease.

Pancreas
> Abdominal digestive gland, extending from duodenum to spleen, containing insulin forming cells.

Palate
> Roof of the mouth.

Palliative
> Mitigating; reducing in severity, noting a method of treating a disease or its symptoms.

Palmar
> Referring to the palm of the hand.

Palpate
> To examine by feeling and pressing with the palms and fingers.

Palpebral
> Relating to an, eyelid or the eyelids.

Papule
> Pimple.

Palsy
> Paralysis.

Paraesthesia
> Abnormal spontaneous sensation, such as a burning, pricking, numbness.

Paralysis
> Loss of power of motion.

Paralysis Agitans
> Shaking paralysis, Parkinson's Disease.

Paraplegia
> Paralysis of legs and lower parts of the body.

Paravertebral

Alongside a vertebra or the spinal column.

Parenchymal

Relating to the specific tissue of a gland or organ.

Paresis

Incomplete paralysis.

Parietal

Pertaining to the walls.

Parkinson's Syndrome

Aggregate symptoms, including raised eyebrows and expressionless face, of paralysis agitans.

Paronychia

Inflammation of structures surrounding the nail or the bone itself of finger or toe.

Paralysis Agitans

Shaking paralysis, Parkinson's Disease.

Paraplegia

Paralysis of legs and lower parts of the body.

Paravertebral

Alongside a vertebra or the spinal column.

Parenchymal

Relating to the specific tissue of a gland or organ.

Paresis

Incomplete paralysis.

Parietal

Pertaining to the walls.

Parkinson's Syndrome

Aggregate symptoms, including raised eyebrows and expressionless face, of paralysis agitans.

Paronychia

Inflammation of structures surrounding the nail or the bone itself of finger or toe.

Passive

Not active.

Past-Pointing

Test of integrity of vestibular apparatus of the ear by rotating person in revolving chair.

Patella

Knee-cap.

Pathology

Branch of medicine which treats of the abnormal tissues in disease.

Pectoral

Relating to the chest.

Pedicle

Stalk or stem forming the attachment of a tumor which is non-sessile, i.e., which does not have a broad base of attachment.

Pellegrini, Stieda's Disease

Bony growth over the internal condyle of the femur, a sequel of stieda's fracture.

Pendulous

Hanging freely or loosely.

Pericardium

Sac enveloping the heart.

Periosteum

Thick, fibrous membrane covering the entire surface of a bone.

Periphery

Outer part or surface.

Peristalsis

Worm-like movement of the gastro-intestinal tract.

Peritoneum

Serous membrane which covers abdominal organs and inner aspect of abdominal walls.

Peritonitis

Inflammation of the peritoneum.

Peroneal

Pertaining to the outer aspects of the leg.

Pes

Foot; foot-like or basal structure or part.

Pes Cavus

Exaggeration of the normal arch of the foot; hollowfoot.

Pes Equinus

Permanent extension of the foot so that only the ball rests on the ground.

Petechial

Relating to minute hemorrhagic spots, of pinpoint to pinhead size, in the skin.

Phalanx

Bone of a finger or toe.

Phlebitis

Inflammation of the veins.

Physiology

Science which treats of functions of different parts of the body.

Physiotherapy

Use of natural forces in the treatment of disease, as in electro-hydro, and aero-therapy, massage, and therapeutic exercises, and use of mechanical devices in mechanotherapy.

Pill-RollingTremor

Tremor in paralysis agitans in the form of circular movement of opposed tips of thumb and index finger.

Pilonidal Cyst

Cyst at the lower end of the spine.

Pisiform

Pea-shaped or pea-sized.

Plantar

Relating to the sole of the foot.

Pleura

Serous membrane which invests lungs and covers inner part of the chest walls (similar to peritoneum in abdominal cavity.)

Pleurisy

Inflammation of the pleura.

Plexus

Network or tangle of nerves.

Plumbism

Lead poisoning.

Pneumoconiosis

Dust disease of the lungs.

Pneumonia

Inflammation of lung substance.

Pneumonoconiosis
Fibrous hardening of the lungs due to irritation caused by inhalation of dust incident to various occupations.

Pneumothorax
Presence of air or gas in the pleural cavity.

Poliomyelitis
Inflammation of the anterior portion of the spinal cord.

Polyp
Pedunculated swelling or outgrowth from a mucus membrane.

Polyuria
Excessive excretion of urine.

Popliteal
Relating to the posterior surface of the knee.

Precordium
Anterior surface of lower part of the thorax.

Pretibial
Relating to anterior portion of the leg.

Proliferative
Excess growth.

Pronate
To rotate the forearm in such a way that the palm of the hand looks backward when the arm is in the anatomical position, or downward when the arm is extended at a right angle with the body.

Prostate
Gland surrounding neck of the male bladder.

Prostatectomy
Removal of all or part of the prostate.

Protuberance
Outgrowth: swelling; knob.

Proximal
Nearest the trunk or point of origin, said of part of an extremity, artery or nerve so situated.

Psychiatrist
Alienist; one who specializes in diseases of the mind.

Psychogenic
Of mental origin or causation.

Ptosis
Drooping down of an eyelid or an organ.

Pubic
One of the bones of the pelvis.

Pulmonic
Relating to the lungs.

Puritis
Itching irritation.

Purulent
Having the appearance of pus or matter.

Pyelitis
Inflammation of a portion of the kidney.

Pyelogram
Roentgenogram of the area of the kidneys and ureter, by use of opaque substances.

Pyogenic
Pus-forming.

R

Radiologist
One skilled in the diagnostic and therapeutic use of x-rays.
Radius
Outer and shorter of the two bones of forearm.
Rales
Sounds of varied character heard on auscultation of the chest in cases of disease of the lungs or bronchi.
Rectum
Terminal portion of the digestive tube.
Reflex
Involuntary or reflected action or movement.
Renal
Pertaining to the kidney.
Resection
Removal of articular ends of one or both bones forming a joint, or of a segment of any part, such as the intestine.
Respiration
Function common to all living plants or animals, consisting in taking in of oxygen and throwing off products of oxidation in the tissues, mainly carbon dioxide and water.
Retina
Inner, nervous tunic of the eyeball, consisting of an outer pigment layer and an inner layer formed by expansion of the optic nerve.
Retrosternal
Behind the sternum.
Rib
One of twenty-four elongated curved bones forming the main portion of bony wall of the chest.
Rhinitis
Inflammation of the nasal mucus membrane.
Roentgenologist
One skilled in the diagnostic and therapeutic use of x-rays.

S

Sacroiliac
Relating to sacrum and ilium, noting articulation between the two bones and associated ligaments.
Sacrum
Triangular bone at the base of the spine.
Sarcoma
Malignant tumor of fibrous tissue or its derivatives.
Scaphoid
Boat-shaped; hollowed.

Scapula

Shoulder-blade.

Sciatica

Painful affection of the sciatic nerve.

Sclerosis

Hardness

Scoliosis

Lateral curvature of the spine.

Scrotum

Sac containing testes.

Semilunar Cartilages

Two intraarticular fibrocartilages of the knee-joint.

Senile

Relating to or characteristic of old age.

Septicemia

Morbid condition due to presence of septic microbes and their poisons in the blood.

Sequela

Morbid condition following as a consequence of another disease.

Sesamoid.

Resembling in size or shape a grain of sesame.

Sequestrum

Piece of dead bone separated from living bone.

Shock

Sudden vital depression due to injury or emotion which makes an untoward depression.

Siderosis

Form of dust disease due to presence of iron dust.

Silicosis

Form of dust disease due to inhalation of stone dust.

Sinusitis

Inflammation of the lining membrane of any sinus, especially of one of the accessory sinuses of the nose.

Spasm

Sudden violent involuntary rigid contraction, due to muscular action.

Sphincter

Orbicular muscle which, when in state of normal contraction, closes one of the orifices of the body.

Spina Bifida

Limited defect in the spinal column consisting in absence of vertebral arches, through which defect spinal membranes protrude.

Spondylolisthesis

Forward subluxation of body of vertebra on vertebra below it or on sacrum.

Sprain

Wrenching of a joint.

Stenosis

Narrowing of an orifice.

Sternoclavicular

Relating to sternum and clavicle, noting an articulation and occasional muscle.

Stricture

Abnormal narrowing of a channel.

Supinate

To turn forearm and hand volar side uppermost.

Suture

Stitch.

Symphysis

Union between two bones by means of fibrocartilage.

Syncope

Fainting.

Syndrome

Complex of symptoms which occur together.

Synovitis

Inflammation of synovial membrane, especially of a joint.

Systole

Period of the heart-beat during which the heart is contracting.

T

Tachycardia

Abnormal increase in rate of the hearts beat, not subsiding on rest, sudden in onset and offset.

Tarsus

Root of the foot or instep.

Temporamandibular

Relating to the temporal bone (bone of the temple) and lower jaw, noting the articulation of the lower jaw.

Tendon

Inelastic fibrous cord or band in which muscle fibers ends and by which muscle is attached to bone or other structure.

Tendosynovitis

Inflammation of the sheath of a tendon.

Tetanus

Lockjaw.

Thorax

Chest, upper part of the trunk between neck and abdomen; it is formed by the twelve dorsal vertebrae, the twelve pairs of ribs, sternum, and muscles and fascias attached to these; it is separated from the abdomen by the diaphragm; it contains chief organs of circulatory and respiratory systems.

Thrombo Angitis Obliterans

Buerger's disease; obliteration of the larger arteries and veins of a limb by thrombi, with subsequent gangrene. See Buerger's Disease.

Thrombophlebitis

Thrombosis with inflammation of the veins.

Thrombosis

Formation of a clot of blood within a blood vessel.

Thyroid

Gland and cartilage of the larynx.

Thyroidectomy

Removal of the thyroid gland.

Tibia

Shin-bone; inner and larger of two bones of the leg.

Tinnitus

Subjective noises (ringing, whistling, booming, etc.) in the ears.

Tonsillitis

Inflammation of a tonsil.

Torticollis

Wry-neck; stiff-neck; spasmodic contraction of muscles of the neck; the head is drawn to one side and usually rotated so that the chin points the other side.

Torsion

Twisting or rotation of a part upon its axis; twisting the cut end of an artery to arrest hemmorhage.

Toxemia

Blood-poisoning.

Toxin

Poison.

Trachea

Windpipe.

Transillumination

Shining light through a translucent part to see if fluid is present.

Trapezius

Muscle extending from back of the head to shoulderbiade; it moves head and shoulder.

Trauma

Wound; injury inflicted usually more or less suddenly by physical agent.

Tremor

Trembling, shaking, loss of equilibrium.

Trephine

Cylindrical or crown saw used for removal of a disc of bone, especially from the skull, or of other firm tissue as that of the cornea.

Triceps

Three-headed muscle extending the forearm. (Covers posterior of upper arm).

Trochanter

One of two bony prominences developed from independent osseous centers near the upper extremity of the thigh bone.

Tubercle

Circumscribed, rounded, solid elevation on the skin, mucus membrane, or surface of an organ; lesion of tuberculosis consisting of a small isolated nodule or aggregation of nodules.

Tuberosity

Broad eminence of bone.

U

Ulcer

Open sore other than a wound.

Ulna

Inner and larger of the two bones of the forearm.

Umbilicus

Navel.

Ununited

Not united or knit, noting an unhealed fracture.

Ureter
Musculomembranous tube leading from kidney to bladder.

Urethra
Membranous tube leading from bladder to external exit.

Urination
The passing of urine.

Urogram
Roentgenogram of any part (kidneys, ureters, bladder) of the urinary tract, with the use of opaque substances.

Urologist
One versed in the branch of medical science which has to do with urine and its modifications in disease.

Urtcaria
Hives.

Uterus
Womb.

V

Varicocele
Varicose veins of the spermatic cord.

Varicose
Dilated, as used in reference to veins.

Varix
Enlarged and tortuous vein, artery, or lymphatic vessel.

Vas
Vessel.

Vasomotor
Regulating mechanism controlling expansion and contraction of blood vessels.

Ventral
Relating to anterior portion.

Ventricular
Relating to a ventricle.

Vertebra
One of thirty-three bones of the spinal column.

Vertex
Crown of the head; topmost point of the vault of the skull.

Vertigo
Dizziness.

Vitiligo
Appearance on the skin of white patches of greater or lesser extent, due to simple loss of pigment without other trophic changes.

Volar
Referring to the palm of the hand.

Z

Zygoma
Strong bar of bone bridging over the depression of the temple; cheek-bone.

————

24678818R00124